Better Homes and Gardens®

OUTDOOR KITCHENS

A DO-IT-YOURSELF GUIDE TO DESIGN AND CONSTRUCTION

Meredith® Books
Des Moines, Iowa

Better Homes and Gardens® Outdoor Kitchens
Editor: Ken Sidey
Writer: Bill LaHay
Senior Associate Design Director: John Eric Seid
Assistant Editor: Harijs Priekulis
Copy Chief: Terri Fredrickson
Copy and Production Editor: Victoria Forlini
Editorial Operations Manager: Karen Schirm
Managers, Book Production: Pam Kvitne,
 Marjorie J. Schenkelberg, Rick von Holdt,
 Mark Weaver
Contributing Copy Editor: Stacey Schildroth
Technical Proofreader: Martin Miller
Contributing Proofreaders: Kathi DiNicola,
 Carolyn Hogan, Gretchen Kauffman, David Krause,
 Terri Krueger, Jina Nelson
Indexer: Donald Glassman
Editorial and Design Assistants: Renee E. McAtee,
 Mary Lee Gavin, Karen McFadden
Field Editors: Andrea Caughey, Stephanie Davis,
 Helen Heitkamp, Nancy E. Ingram

Additional Editorial and Design Contributions from
Abramowitz, Staub & Associates, Inc.
Designer: Tim Abramowitz
Editor: Catherine M. Staub

Art Rep Services
Director: Chip Nadeau
Designer: lk Design
Illustrator: Shawn Wallace

Meredith® Books
Editor in Chief: Linda Raglan Cunningham
Design Director: Matt Strelecki
Executive Editor, Gardening and Home Improvement:
 Benjamin W. Allen
Executive Editor, Home Improvement: Larry Erickson

Publisher: James D. Blume
Executive Director, Marketing: Jeffrey Myers
Executive Director, New Business Development:
 Todd M. Davis
Executive Director, Sales: Ken Zagor
Director, Operations: George A. Susral
Director, Production: Douglas M. Johnston
Business Director: Jim Leonard

Vice President and General Manager: Douglas J. Guendel

Meredith Publishing Group
President, Publishing Group: Stephen M. Lacy
Vice President-Publishing Director: Bob Mate

Meredith Corporation
Chairman and Chief Executive Officer: William T. Kerr

In Memoriam: E. T. Meredith III (1933-2003)

Thanks to
The Outdoor Kitchen Store, Tampa, FL

Photographers
(Photographers credited may retain copyright ©
 to the listed photographs.)
L = Left, R = Right, C = Center, B = Bottom,
 T = Top

Russell Abraham: 4B, 9B, 49BR
Ron Blakely: 16B
Crandall & Crandall: 8B, 12, 17B, 29T, 49T, 49BL
Fire Magic Co.: 32T
Ed Gohlich: Cover, 11, 23T, 25T, 82, 86, 87
Jay Graham: 38, 50, 88, 92, 93
Greenleaf Publishing: 137
Image Studios: 14, 15, 110, 113, 114, 115, 117, 121, 126,
 138, 140, 144, 146, 154, 156
Jenifer Jordan: 20B, 46, 47
Ann Reilly/Positive Images: 10B, 18T
Solaire: 32B
William Stites: 17T, 22, 24, 42, 76, 80, 81, 100, 104,
 105, 106,
Deidra Walpole Photography: 16T, 19, 45TL, 45TR,
 45BL, 45BR
Weber-Stephen Products Co.: 33
Woollybugger Studios: 10T

Project Designers
Lisa Chestnut: 64–69
Garbini and Garbini: 52–57
Marlen Kemmet: 94–99
Peter Koenig: 88–93
Knudson Gloss Architects/Planners: 58–63; 64–69
Small & Rossell Landscape Architects: 70–75
Jim Sneed/Bokal Kelly-Markham: 52–57
Chip Vogel/Interior Spaces: 106–109
Bob Wheelington: 82–87

Copyright © 2004 by Meredith Corporation,
 Des Moines, Iowa. First Edition.
All rights reserved. Printed in the United States
 of America.
Library of Congress Control Number: 2003106436
ISBN: 0-696-21756-2

All of us at Meredith® Books are dedicated to
providing you with the information and ideas you
need to enhance your home and garden. We welcome
your comments and suggestions. Write to us at:
Meredith Books
Home Improvement Books Department
1716 Locust St.
Des Moines, IA 50309–3023

If you would like to purchase any of our home
improvement, gardening, cooking, crafts, or home
decorating and design books, check wherever quality
books are sold. Or visit us at: bhgbooks.com

TABLE OF CONTENTS

CHAPTER 1
ASSESSING YOUR NEEDS 7
A Table for How Many? 8
Writing Your Menu 9
What About the Weather? 10

CHAPTER 2
PLANNING YOUR KITCHEN 13
Creating a Layout 14
Judging the Terrain and Climate ... 18
Principles of Kitchen Design 20
Your Design Process 30
Product Guide 32
Working with Contractors 35

CHAPTER 3
DESIGN GALLERY 39
Fiesta Colors 40
Family Oasis 41
Classical Gas 42
Hideaway Haven 43
Heat Is On 44
Grand Islands 45
Under Cover 46
Staying Connected 48

CHAPTER 4
KITCHENS YOU CAN BUILD 51
Classic Brick Courtyard 52
Under the Big Top 58

Rock Solid 64
Fire and Shelter 70
Poolside Dining 76
Dining Center Stage 82
All the Angles 88
Out in the Woods 94
Gimme Shelter 100
A Basic Built-in 106

CHAPTER 5
CONSTRUCTION BASICS 110
Working with Concrete 112
Brick Paver Patios 123
Building Concrete Block Walls 126
Adding Brick or Stone Veneer 133
Building Brick Walls 134
Working with Ceramic Tile 138
Deck-Building Basics 144
Framing with Wood 150
Framing with Metal 153
Utility Connections 154

CHAPTER 6
ENJOYING YOUR KITCHEN 158
Care and Maintenance 160
Cooking in Your Outdoor Kitchen . 162
All-Time Favorite Grilling Recipes . 164

Glossary 170
Index 172
Resources 175

MOVING THE KITCHEN OUTDOORS

Kitchens have long been more than just a place to cook. They have served as a place of warmth, a gathering room for family, an offer of hospitality. Today's homeowners expect that, and more. They demand a degree of versatility from a kitchen that they would never expect from any other space in the house. Little surprise, then, that the growing popularity of outdoor kitchens is about much more than grilling burgers on the patio.

Gone are the rusted charcoal grill and the splinter-happy picnic table of past generations. In their place, gleaming stainless-steel built-ins provide the means to cook and serve a smorgasbord of smoke-flavored favorites. Properly designed and built, filled with fixtures and amenities, today's outdoor kitchens let you feast in the open air with all the convenience

▼ The best outdoor kitchen designs combine function, a dining area, privacy, and even a venue for entertaining.

▲ Outdoor cooking can be as ambitious as you want it to be. This island has a gas burner and a prep sink for canning fruits and vegetables.

of an enclosed room. Like the most elegant of formal dinners, cooking and eating outdoors can be an enjoyable ritual for family and friends, no matter what's on the menu.

Form and function

However simple you want your outdoor kitchen to be, you'll be faced with hundreds of decisions, ranging from where and how big to build to how many Btus you really need in a grill burner—or whether you even want to swap your charcoal for gas fuel in the first place. The opening chapter, "Assessing Your Needs," addresses these questions, helping you recognize how your site, budget, regional climate, family size, cooking preferences, and entertaining style all factor into the best possible design. In Chapter Two, "Planning

Your Kitchen," you'll find planning strategies that help you target the specific features most likely to give you the kitchen you want. Will you attach the kitchen to the home's exterior or build a freestanding version? How should storage be organized? Do you want a side burner, a prep sink, or a fridge, and if so, what's involved in bringing gas, water, and electricity to the cooking station? You'll also find a guide to help you shop for the latest in grills and other outdoor cooking products.

Of course there's more than just function to consider. That's why Chapter Three offers a "Design Gallery" of great-looking outdoor kitchens, each offering inspiration for adding features to your own kitchen plans.

Under construction

Then there's the actual building process. The series of 10 "Kitchens You Can Build" shows what's needed to bring these beautiful, functional designs to life in your yard. The chapter on "Construction Basics" teaches you the best materials and techniques for the job, whether you use that knowledge to hire a contractor or roll up your sleeves and tackle the work yourself.

You'll even find some help for enjoying your new outdoor kitchen—a selection of favorite grilling recipes and cooking tips from the Better Homes and Gardens® Test Kitchen. From planning and dreaming to licking your fingers, here's all you need for your new outdoor kitchen.

◄ Some outdoor kitchens take a supporting role. Here the kitchen is situated to provide easy access to refreshments after a swim.

ASSESSING YOUR NEEDS

Are you sold on the concept of the outdoor kitchen and eager to create your own? You can start with a no-limits wish list, but it's important to stay focused. Just like an interior remodeling project, an outdoor kitchen can evolve in many directions within a wide range of budgets. If it's instant results you're after, you can purchase a portable modular kitchen cart for $2,500, but splurge on custom built-ins with a shelter structure and extensive landscaping and you can spend $50,000 before you flip your first burger. Rather than let your lot size, budget, or available amenities drive your design, plan around how you want to use the kitchen. This can involve the number of persons in your household, the type of cooking you intend to do, or how often you're likely to use the space for entertaining large groups. Even if you're skilled and ambitious enough to do the actual building, this early concept stage will likely benefit from professional design services. You want to avoid investing time and money in a poorly planned and designed building or remodeling project that results in a long "If only . . ." list staring you in the face after it's finished. Focus on the function you need, and the design will evolve accordingly.

A TABLE FOR HOW MANY?

Versatile outdoor kitchens receive the most use. These are spaces capable of handling a quiet family dinner or a holiday bash for several dozen close friends. You'll need to establish a range of likely scenarios to come up with a workable plan that meets your various needs. As long as the numbers spread is moderate, the work core of the kitchen—where the grill sits and where food is prepared—doesn't have to change drastically to accommodate groups of different sizes. Even more critical are the overall social area of the patio or deck and your willingness to bring in extra seating when it's required. Many homeowners want at least a grill, a refrigerator, and perhaps a prep sink in their outdoor kitchen but opt to do without other amenities they'd never dream of omitting in their main kitchen. Plan your must-have core elements around how you anticipate using your space. If the grill is too small to cook all the food at once, or if the limited storage capacity of your undercounter refrigerator has you constantly traipsing indoors for essentials, then the energy, time, and money you've put into your outdoor kitchen won't seem well spent. So first things first: Make a thoughtful commitment to a minimum level of function to ensure a worthwhile project.

► This site features separate zones for the food prep and dining areas. Small groups can migrate easily as the meal evolves, and large groups can mingle more casually back and forth at a party. Flexibility is essential for outdoor spaces.

WRITING YOUR MENU

Your second consideration should be what type of cooking you want to do in your outdoor space. Again, focus should be on versatility and meeting your everyday needs, not covering a contingency of unlikely "what if?" scenarios. Consider the following:

■ Creating a casual dining atmosphere is what outdoor kitchens do best, so play to their strengths. Save temperamental or delicate dishes for a controlled indoor setting, and indulge in simpler cuisine that's more at home outside.

■ If you're setting up a poolside snack center for kids, essentials can be as basic as a refrigerator for soft drinks, a microwave oven, and a small work counter with a sink for simple food prep and cleanup.

■ To make full dinners for family and friends, you'll likely want a built-in grill and one or two auxiliary burners, plus a bigger refrigerator and a sizable island for preparing and serving food.

■ Rotisserie ovens or meat smokers are both naturals for an outdoor kitchen and should be considered as you formulate your early plans.

That still leaves a pretty big culinary universe, one that combines plenty of flavors, textures, and colors to make great dishes. Of course this might mean duplicating some of the appliances in your main kitchen and providing weather-resistant installations for them, but if it's a self-contained outdoor cooking center you want and your budget is big enough to handle the extra costs, the options are there.

▲ Visualizing the menus for your outdoor cooking and dining makes planning a kitchen that has what you need easier.

◄ With a grill, side burner, and refrigerator, this open-air kitchen lets the homeowner prepare an entire meal conveniently.

WHAT ABOUT THE WEATHER?

Climate issues are covered in more detail in the planning section. For now, do a quick review of the weather conditions you're up against. Chart the months that are most likely to be included in your outdoor cooking season, then make some notes about the following climatic factors:

- Average seasonal temperatures.
- Typical frequency and intensity of rainfall.
- Sunlight patterns at the site for various times of the year.
- Prevailing wind conditions.

If rain means you won't want to be outdoors anyway, then plan for protection of the kitchen elements and not necessarily for a roof to keep you dry. Sun and wind are a different story; assume they'll both be factors when you're using the kitchen. Other site features, such as a

▼ Rain is the bane of the outdoor chef. Plan for some cover under a patio umbrella, an awning, or a permanent roof.

▲ Winter temperatures may be too cold for dining outside, but you can still fire up a grill to cook, even with snow on the ground.

perimeter fence or even the house itself, might be allies in taming these problems. In that case, your kitchen design can be less complicated. All of these factors focus on permanent installations, which you'll see aren't the only options. You can build or buy modular components for an outdoor kitchen, mounted on casters for portability, that let you set things up as needed when weather conditions are favorable.

◀ A roof over your head provides protection from sun as well as rain. Consider sunlight patterns as you plan your kitchen layout.

ACCESS FOR ALL

Thanks to legislation such as the Americans with Disabilities Act (ADA), public and commercial buildings now feature designs that make them more accessible to wheelchair users and others whose mobility might be limited. But access issues aren't just about doorways and ramps. During the past several decades, new approaches to access have spawned the term universal design and have focused on better ergonomics, ease of use, and access for everyone. A private residence is not subject to the same legal mandates as a public building, but making access and usability top priorities in your outdoor kitchen design will ensure that it's comfortable for anyone to use. Here are some principles you can apply:

- Store frequently used items on hooks or open shelves at heights between 18 and 60 inches above the ground.
- Grill and burner controls should be front-mounted, but out of the reach of children.
- Use sliding shelves and drawers to make stored items more accessible.
- Plan clearances that can accommodate a wheelchair: 36-inch aisles or doorways; 30-inch minimum height under a sink or counter; a 5-foot square area to turn around; no slopes steeper than 10 degrees; and no gaps or abrupt transitions in floor.

PLANNING YOUR KITCHEN

Spontaneity might be great for heartfelt wedding toasts and improvisational comedy, but when it comes to building projects, good planning rules the day. The early stages of daydreaming and imagining your new outdoor kitchen should give your thoughts the appropriate opportunity to wander, but at some point all those vague notions have to become specific realities. That gleaming new grill needs a certain amount of space, you've got some excavating to do for the slab and retaining wall, and the wiring for your undercounter fridge has to come from somewhere. These are the details you'll sort out during the planning stage. If you haven't already recruited some help from a professional designer, this is a good time to bring one on board, if only to resolve some of the technical issues and to offer a fresh perspective.

CREATING A LAYOUT

▲ A simple scale drawing will tell you exactly what will fit on your site.

After you've assessed your general needs, consider the features you want in an outdoor kitchen. Match your wish list, which at this stage is at least part fantasy, to the realities of building the actual project. Budget considerations loom large at this point, but until you sort out more of the specifics, it won't do much good to estimate the costs you're facing. Like any building project, an outdoor kitchen must be developed in a sequence of individual steps, working from the most general to the most specific. Site evaluation is the first step.

Start by creating a simple layout of your potential sites on graph paper. (Use ¼-inch graph paper and draw to the standard architectural scale of ¼ inch equals one foot.) The scale of this layout should allow you to represent the area of the entire backyard and the rear sections of the house in an overhead view similar to a floor plan. In the first layout, include existing patios, planters, walkways,

▶ Don't stop with just one plan. Do at least three drawings with different layouts, then combine the best features or pick a favorite. If you push beyond your first, most obvious ideas, you'll likely come up with good alternatives.

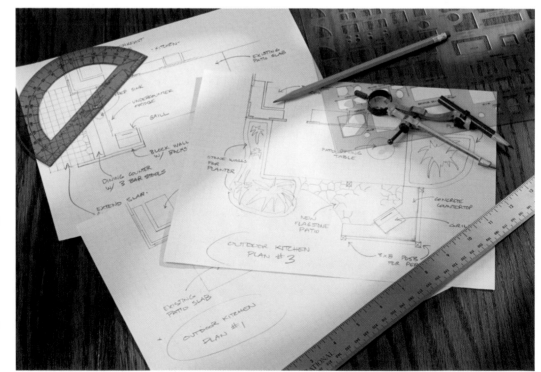

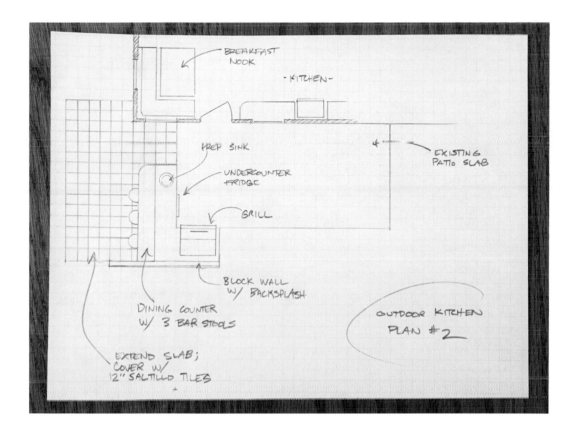

Once you've settled on a plan you like, run it by the local building officials who will have to approve the design and issue the permit. They can do a quick assessment and let you know what code issues will be involved with the project.

trees, or any other feature that might affect the design for your kitchen area—even if it's an element you want to remove. Next create two or three rough sketches of possible plans for the kitchen, keeping them to scale so you get an accurate sense of what can fit in your yard. You may arrive at a workable plan with your first try, but don't stop there. Creating one or two alternates is likely to engender some good ideas that didn't surface on your first round. As you sketch different options, think of the outdoor kitchen as a fixed room, much like an interior space, so you can keep the functional elements concentrated into a convenient work core.

More often than not, the back entry of the house will connect directly to the main kitchen or an adjacent space, such as a family room. With this in mind, position your outdoor kitchen to allow for reasonably easy access and a fairly direct traffic route from the house. It's common for many homeowners to attach their outdoor kitchen directly to an exterior wall of the main kitchen. This certainly offers convenience, especially if a pass-through window is placed in the common wall so items can be handed directly between the two areas. It also makes it simpler to install the necessary utility lines (electric, gas, and water), to buffer the space from too much sun or wind, or to extend the roof over the outdoor kitchen. (See "Location, Location" on page 17 for a more detailed accounting of the pros and cons of attached and freestanding outdoor kitchens.)

But these aren't the only things to consider. You might want a more distant location that takes advantage of a great view or that's more convenient to some other feature, such as a backyard swimming pool or a freestanding deck. The larger your yard, the more likely it is that a detached outdoor kitchen will be useful. In order to provide convenience at a more remote location, the project should be more self-contained. An outdoor cooking center just outside the kitchen door won't suffer much functionally if it doesn't include its own refrigerator, but locate it 40 feet away and you'll find that feature, as well as other cooking and storage functions, becomes more critical.

▲ Freestanding kitchens typically allow several design options, but if they are self-contained enough to be convenient, plan on higher costs.

▶ The compact size of this covered patio demands a cooking center to the side, so the main area is open for dining and sitting.

LOCATION, LOCATION

Among the first big decisions you'll have to make about your outdoor kitchen is whether it will be attached to the house or freestanding. Here's a quick profile of what each option entails:

An outdoor kitchen attached to the home:

■ Gains a shelter advantage from existing walls and/or roof.

■ Makes utility connections easier and less expensive.

■ Can often have more amenities, such as storage or appliances.

■ Offers convenience if located just outside the main kitchen.

■ Requires a powered vent to direct grilling smoke away from indoors.

■ Loses some of the ambience of an outdoor retreat.

A freestanding outdoor kitchen:

■ Typically involves more structural work for the foundation and fixtures.

■ Requires more work for utility connections.

■ Will be more exposed to inclement weather.

■ Offers more options for site placement, design, and total area.

■ Enhances other detached outdoor areas, such as pools or decks.

■ Provides a more direct and casual outdoor experience.

JUDGING THE TERRAIN AND CLIMATE

▲ A wood deck is often the best option for building on slopes and uneven terrain where a flat concrete slab isn't practical. Decks offer more flexibility in design; they easily accommodate multiple levels and unusual shapes.

▼ Protection from the weather doesn't have to involve complex or expensive features. Here an awning offers shelter from the sun and rain.

Not everyone has a backyard site that's construction-friendly. Level ground makes it easier to create structural elements, such as a concrete slab or a block wall, while a sloped or unfriendly site will require a different strategy for the foundation.

Rough terrain can still provide an ideal spot for the kitchen; it will simply take a different approach to the early building stages and perhaps some additional expense. It might mean the best option for the main platform is a wood deck supported by individual concrete piers or

that a slab floor is possible but must be contained within a perimeter wall foundation. Of course if you already have a patio, you may be able to add the kitchen fixtures such as a grill, countertops, and storage base.

A sloped site introduces other issues as well. If you build on the upper levels, you may lose privacy or end up with the kitchen exposed to excess wind or other climatic conditions. Build on low ground and you'll have to deal with drainage and water runoff.

As you may have guessed by now, there is no one best strategy for choosing the site of your outdoor kitchen. The floor plan of your home, the topography of the yard, and your plans for using the kitchen must all factor into the design. Whatever cannot be changed must be accommodated, particularly when faced with climatic factors. Designing for weather involves more than just protection from the rain, though that's usually the first objective. Windbreaks can be added, either through fencing and similar structures or via tempered glass panels that retain the views you want. Protection from harsh sun can and often should come from a variety of sources—a permanent roof or retractable awning, trees, roll-up shades, or blinds fitted to glass windbreak panels. If mosquitoes, flies, or other insects are a problem, consider a screened room for dining as one of the permanent structures for your kitchen.

Become familiar with the common weather patterns for the "microclimate" in your yard, start taking notes. Keep track of the seasonal temperatures, prevailing winds, the location and angle of the sun at different times of the year, and average rainfall. These conditions can determine everything from the best orientation for the kitchen to what type of shelter you'll need. Remember that although built-in features and shelter structures add to the project cost, they'll also extend the season for outdoor cooking and dining. If you want the option of year-round use and live in a northern state where snow accumulation and frigid temperatures are part of your winter weather, you'll need a fairly elaborate shelter equipped with heat, protective walls, and a roof.

SITE CHECKLIST

Consider these factors when selecting the location for your outdoor kitchen:

- Plan for good traffic flow to and from the house, both from the kitchen itself and from other outdoor areas.
- Aim for convenient access to utility connections (water, gas, and electric).
- If possible, select level terrain so it's easier to construct a foundation.
- Don't ignore drainage issues. Stay out of the path of storm-water runoff.
- Try to avoid prevailing winds or harsh sun; plan protective features if necessary.
- If there's a view worth preserving, site the kitchen accordingly.

PRINCIPLES OF KITCHEN DESIGN

As a rule, outdoor kitchens are neither fully equipped nor used on a daily basis, so they usually don't involve the complexity of a home's main indoor kitchen. Still, there are basic functional categories that you'll want to consider from mainstream kitchen design—storage, food preparation, cooking, dining, and cleanup. Not all of these functions are required of an

▲ An outdoor sink makes it easier to prepare salads and side dishes. That doesn't always require plumbing runs. A garden hose can supply water, and runoff can be collected in an under-counter reservoir.

▶ Counter area near the grill is a must for safety and convenience. You need landing space for hot dishes or pans, and room to fill plates with food.

outdoor kitchen, especially if you only want a grilling station, but it's best to include as many as you can during the initial planning stages. If you end up wanting a simpler or more streamlined design, you can always drop the extraneous features.

You won't get far in a discussion of kitchen design without hearing the word "layout." This term refers to the overall arrangement of the kitchen, from its size and basic shape to the placement of cabinets, appliances, and other large items. One of the tried-and-true principles of layout strategy is the work triangle—the space connecting the stove, refrigerator, and sink. Among certified professional kitchen designers, this subspace merits its own rules that make a kitchen efficient to work in but not cramped. Generally the length of each leg of the triangle should be greater than 4 feet but less than 9 feet. Recently, however, the trend in kitchen layouts has become more flexible, blending art and science. With islands, prep sinks, duplicate appliances, and other new features now commonplace, the insistence on a defined work triangle is less rigid. It's more likely that a new kitchen will be set up with several workstations or activity zones that concentrate specific functions in one spot.

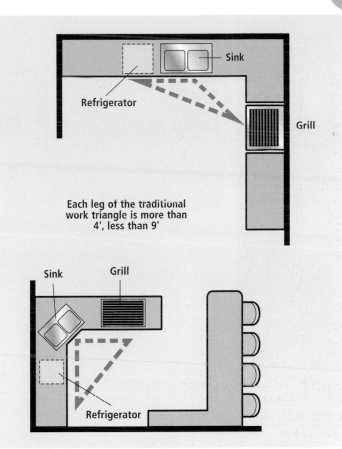

Each leg of the traditional work triangle is more than 4', less than 9'

▲ The work triangle—an imaginary outline connecting the sink, refrigerator, and stove—is a basic principle of indoor kitchen design that can be adapted for outdoor installations.

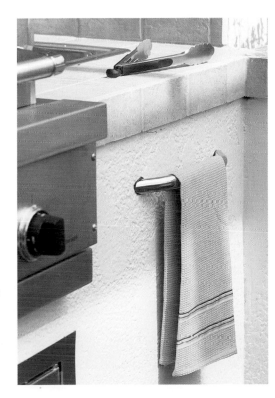

▶ When you're focused on big things such as the grill, it's easy to overlook the small stuff. Don't forget towel bars, hooks, and hangers for convenience.

FIVE FUNCTIONAL CATEGORIES

Likewise, the agenda for outdoor kitchens has gained some flexibility. A good way to start your planning is to focus on the individual tasks you'll perform in the space. In other words, imagine what the kitchen will do, not what it will have. A typical use of an outdoor kitchen might involve bringing out raw ingredients and prepared foods (and needing somewhere to set them), cutting and rinsing foods, placing aside hot pans or utensils while cooking, setting out the food when it's ready, and cleaning everything up after the meal is over. Once you've established how many of these functions you want your kitchen to handle, it's much easier to determine the specific features necessary to get the job done. If you jump ahead to that must-have built-in grill or fancy refrigerator without thinking through the actual preparation of a meal, you may find yourself with makeshift solutions for everyday needs, such as counter space for food or hot pans, storage for paper towels and cooking supplies, and other necessities. That said, here's a look at five basic

■ Good storage is as much about access as it is about volume. Whether it's a convenient spot for a refrigerator or a forward-tilt mount for the propane tank, make sure you can get at the stuff you need.

functional categories and how they factor into an outdoor kitchen:

Storage

Cold storage of beverages is a common feature for an outdoor kitchen. A compact undercounter refrigerator can often handle the task, and if a weekend party or big dinner event claims all the refrigerator space for food storage, use ice chests or plastic tubs to keep soft drinks and beer chilled. Dry storage should be created for grilling utensils, cleaning supplies, paper goods, and other items that won't spoil or attract animals. Finally, consider specialty items such as a portable tabletop burner, extra propane tanks, and other accessories that you might want to store close at hand. Wood cabinetry (designed specifically for outdoor use) or enclosures inside

▲ If countertop area isn't large enough to give you sufficient work space, add a retractable surface such as this sliding granite shelf.

a masonry surround are the most common solutions for storage. Plan for the everyday uses you anticipate and bring in temporary reinforcements (a portable kitchen cart, for example) for special occasions. Odds are you won't be able to anticipate every situation anyway, so stay flexible for the exceptions.

Food preparation

First and foremost you need a work surface that's large enough, that's easy to keep clean, and that can stand up to the elements. The premium choice for many homeowners is a granite slab or its manufactured cousin known as engineered quartz. When polished on the face and edges, these materials provide great-looking and durable work surfaces. Granite

slabs must be periodically sealed with mineral oil but otherwise are a virtually maintenance-free material. Engineered quartz (sold under brand names such as DuPont Zodiaq, Silestone, and Crystallite) has properties similar to granite, though it's composed partially of plastic binder resins, making it vulnerable to extreme heat. On the plus side, its nonporous surface doesn't require sealing. Both products must be professionally fabricated and installed, and costs can run as high as $100 to $200 per square foot for the pricier varieties. Other slab products to consider are marble, slate, or concrete (either prefabricated or poured-in-place). The cost for these materials is typically lower, but trade-offs in durability and maintenance requirements are minuses.

◄ Most grill makers also produce storage cabinets and drawers for outdoor use. The stainless-steel construction of this unit ensures easier cleaning.

Ceramic tile is another popular choice for outdoor surfaces, but the grout lines require periodic maintenance to keep them clean and sealed. Tile comes in numerous design and color choices, and if you're willing to get your hands dirty and rent a few specialty tools, you might be able to install it yourself. When shopping for tile be sure to specify vitreous or impervious tile, which are both watertight and can be used outside without concern for damage from freeze/thaw cycles. (Nonvitreous and semivitreous tiles absorb moisture and are for interior use only.) Don't use unglazed tile; it requires regular applications of sealant and will

■ Some tiles come with a weathered look, just right for use outdoors. If they are glazed and rated for wet environments, they'll keep their good looks for many years.

not perform as well as glazed tile.

Some surfaces common in indoor kitchens, such as plastic laminate or solid-surface countertops, should not be used unless they are protected from rain and direct sun. Seams on laminate countertops will often degrade if saturated with water, and solid-surface materials are not designed for prolonged exterior exposure. Stainless steel holds up well and is easy to clean, and the same metal fabricators that outfit local restaurants can make a countertop for you. Despite its name, however, stainless steel will eventually corrode in oceanfront environments, so if you live on or near the beach, stay with a stone or ceramic tile surface. Also keep in mind that wood or plastic cutting boards still represent a better option for

direct contact with food, so you should keep one or two on hand.

Aside from a work surface, a prep sink (with faucet) ranks among the more useful amenities in an outdoor kitchen. You can use it to fill pots for cooking, clean fruits and vegetables, and rinse dishes or cooking utensils. This feature adds considerable cost and complexity to the kitchen, especially in northern climates where the water supply line must be protected from freezing. Typically only a cold water line is installed. In some regions it must be buried 4 or 5 feet underground, then heavily insulated or even heated with an electric wire wrap where it emerges to connect to the faucet. (An alternate approach is to install the line with an indoor valve—usually in the basement—so it can be drained before each winter.) A waste line must tie into your home's main drainage system or empty into a dry well.

If a fully functional prep sink is on your wish list, an outdoor kitchen connected directly to your home's exterior will simplify the installation. If a detached site works better but you want to avoid the higher costs of a fully functional sink installation, there are simpler options. Some homeowners fit a garden hose connection to the back of the kitchen surround or island to hook up the water supply. (It helps if you can route the garden hose discreetly behind the kitchen.) Even then, you still have drainage options to consider. While a few sites might lend themselves to a simple open drain line to discharge the spent water, many local codes don't allow this. Unless the terrain is sloped to prevent problems from water runoff, it's not a good solution anyway. A better approach is to provide a portable gray-water reservoir (a 5- to 15-gallon plastic tub, for example) underneath the sink and empty it periodically as required. If you avoid using chemicals such as harsh cleaning agents at the sink, you can use the gray water to irrigate outdoor plants.

■ If counter space is scarce, consider installing just a bar sink. They're small but get the job done.

▲ Built-in grills are favored for their clean look, large capacity, and the convenience of using piped-in natural gas for fuel. This model has an integral side burner and can be fitted with a rotisserie for roasting large cuts of meat.

charcoal or manufactured briquettes. Grills that use liquid propane or natural gas, though, are much more popular for the built-in applications common in outdoor kitchens. Virtually all higher quality gas grills feature ceramic briquettes fitted between the meat grids above and the burner element below. These ceramic disks prevent flame flare-ups and protect the burner from the corrosive effects of hot grease and salts. In addition they accumulate oils and fats, and as they are heated their smoke imparts flavor to the grilled meats, adding the charbroiled flavor associated with charcoal cooking. (For more on grill types and features, see pages 160–163.) Whatever grill type or size you choose, be sure to consider the possibility of mechanical ventilation through a vent hood. This is often a requirement for outdoor kitchens attached to the house, but even freestanding units might warrant such a feature.

Cooking

Cooking food is at the heart of the outdoor kitchen, but the approach is different from that of indoor cooking. It's hard to be fussy outdoors. Nuanced culinary touches are difficult to manage in a semicontrolled climate, so simple recipes with robust flavors rule the day. Finger foods move to the top of the menu. It's this simplicity associated with outdoor cuisine, a fundamental hands-on experience that harkens back to more primitive times, that drives the design of today's outdoor kitchen.

The core, or hearth, of these modern kitchens is the grill. Wood-burning ovens, open fire pits with hand-crank spits, or smokers are sometime included as well, but the grill usually takes center stage. If you are a traditionalist, you'll insist on cooking with hardwood lump

▲ Consider what you'll be cooking on the grill to guide your choice of features.

Many grills come with rotisseries as standard or optional equipment for roasting whole chickens or large cuts of meat. In addition at least one standard burner can help with cooking vegetables or side dishes. Other useful cooking devices are meat smokers and the large deep fryers that run on propane. These tend to be used intermittently, so you might want to add portable rather than installed units. Make sure there's enough space around the built-in elements to set them up and use them if they're stored elsewhere.

■ Techniques for cooking outdoors can vary from the primitive simplicity of an open fire pit (above), modernized here with a rotisserie, to a high-tech gas burner (left) wrapped in gleaming stainless steel. If you have room, build some options into your kitchen to suit the foods you want to cook.

▼ For open-air enthusiasts, outdoor cooking goes beyond flipping burgers. Wood-burning ovens are a favorite for pizza, offering flavors no indoor oven can rival.

FIVE FUNCTIONAL CATEGORIES (CONTINUED)

Dining

There's more latitude for dining arrangements than almost any other functional aspect of outdoor kitchens. By far the most flexible arrangement is a freestanding patio dining set; all you need is the space on your deck or patio to set it up. Some outdoor kitchens incorporate a built-in countertop bar that can seat a few diners. If you plan for this feature, keep it well away from the grill.

▲ Storage should be simple. Keep everyday items within reach by using open racks.

▲ Dining counters are perfect for outdoor kitchens. They let diners mingle with the cook and are space-efficient.

Whatever built-in features are in your kitchen, include a freestanding dining set, alloting a space at least 8×8 feet square to accommodate it. Envision the traffic patterns likely to occur and allow for them so diners can get to and from the table without interfering with activity at the cooking center. And unless you've got a powerful vent hood that captures all the smoke from your grill, keep the dining area at a slight distance so wayward cooking fumes don't ruin an otherwise good meal.

▲ A cutout in this granite countertop houses a restaurant-style condiments tray, equipped to turn any burger into a work of culinary art.

Cleanup

Some of the same components that help with food preparation also come in handy for cleanup chores. A large work surface gives you room to collect dirty dishes or consolidate and package leftover food. The prep sink, though it's likely not large enough for hand-washing dishes, can be used to rinse the worst mess off the plates before you bring them inside. (If you opt for a more temporary drainage system, such as the gray-water tank discussed earlier, you'll have to exercise some care in what you put down the sink.) Other than these features, the two best cleanup elements you can include are a bay to house a trash receptacle and a bin for empty bottles, cans, and other recyclables.

▲ Having a permanent shelter overhead opens up an entire vista of options for an outdoor kitchen. This installation houses a dishwasher and plenty of storage for dishes, making it nearly as self-contained as the main kitchen.

◀ A prep sink is key to cleaning produce and your hands while cooking, but it will also speed the cleanup process if you want to rinse dirty dishes before hauling them inside.

YOUR DESIGN PROCESS

The final considerations for your design process should include site-specific elements such as the finish materials on your home's exterior and personal preferences for the colors and textures you want in the project. Also take into account how much your budget allows for materials and outside help, such as additional design or construction services.

The aesthetics of your home's exterior should be considered when designing your outdoor kitchen. Whatever you build should be stylistically compatible with existing features. This requirement applies especially to outdoor kitchens that are attached, but don't assume you have to mimic every element. Echoing a few key details of your house—a brick base or prominent trim piece, for example—can visually tie an outdoor structure to the house.

▼ **The closer the outdoor kitchen is to the house, the more the design should be tailored to match features on the home's exterior.**

Now that you've got a good understanding of how to plan your kitchen, you can mark its rough location with stakes and create a few sketches of the overall site and kitchen layout. If you have an existing patio where the cooking center will go, use tape or cardboard templates on the ground to indicate the layout. For the next step, you'll need to select the specific built-in items you want to include—grill, sink, appliances, and additional amenities—so you can develop scaled drawings on graph paper with all of the necessary dimensions on hand.

If creating detailed drawings for your project exceeds your skill level or if you decide you want some help at this stage, contact local landscape architects or design firms and work with them to fill in the specifics. You'll already have all or most of the basic ingredients determined; a good designer will combine your requests and add a few suggestions to develop a design package tailored to your specific needs. Some firms offer designing and building services; others will do only the design work and will refer you to a landscaper or other contractor for the actual construction. Of course, you can do much or all of the building work yourself—the instructions in the following sections will help you get started.

▲ An outdoor kitchen is typically only one element among many in a backyard, so the design has to work in context. Here, the mix includes two pergolas, a pool, a concrete patio, and the lawn area.

◄ The design process for an outdoor space has to consider everything about the site, from the prevailing wind direction to the views you want. A strong focal point, like this fire pit, helps create a sense of intimacy, even in the great outdoors.

PRODUCT GUIDE

In most outdoor kitchens, the grill is the most expensive single item purchased, and the wide variety of features and technologies offered by manufacturers can make the choice seem overwhelming. Here are some things to consider when looking:

Focus on the food, not the grill. What you cook and how you like to cook it will help determine the best grill for you. If steak seared to perfection is your priority, a grill with a high-Btu output or with infrared burners will serve you best. Want to roast large birds? Look for a rotisserie feature with a rear-mounted infrared burner. Some foods, such as pork, require high initial heat for searing followed by lower heat for thorough cooking; fish generally requires lower temperatures. In both cases a conventional gas burner works nicely. The best grills typically offer several options for cooking methods, so you don't have to trade versatility for performance.

Next consider the fuel for the grill. Hard-piped natural gas is the most convenient and the

▼ Some manufacturers offer modular designs that let you specify the burners you want. This grill has a standard gas convection burner on one side, with infrared burners on the other side and the back.

▲ An infrared rotisserie burner provides better results for large roasts or whole birds.

most common fuel for built-in grills. Liquid propane gas (LP), typically stored in 20-pound cylinders, is used more widely than any other outdoor cooking fuel. It works well for remote locations or stand-alone outdoor kitchens You can have a larger permanent storage tank installed. If you're a traditionalist, there are still plenty of charcoal-burning units available. A new option offered with many LP grills is an accessory pan that lets you cook with charcoal as well as propane.

The hardware

Higher quality materials and closer attention to detail typically translate into better cooking. Some choices you will face are about durability and good looks; others are about functionality and cooking efficiency.

The housing is what you see first. Most lower-priced grills feature enameled-steel housings, which used to be the industry standard. Improved paint technologies enable

CHAPTER 2

these products to last longer than they used to, but eventually they will rust out. Nowadays the trend is toward more durable alternates: cast aluminum and stainless steel. While both of these materials will corrode slightly in harsh oceanside environments, under most circumstances they'll survive to serve the next generation of backyard chefs. Aluminum units typically are painted; those with thick shells (about ¼ inch) tend to maintain their looks better than those with thinner walls. Stainless steel is by far the most popular material, both for its high-end looks and its low maintenance requirements. (An occasional blast from a garden hose, followed by a towel wipe, is all it usually needs.) Stainless steel comes in different grades and alloys; you'll find Type 304 or Type 316 on most grills. Better-quality grills may use thicker gauge stainless steel or a #321 alloy, and the fit-and-finish details are typically nicer.

For most grills, it's what's inside that counts— the burner units and the grates are where the food meets the fire, and that's where to look for quality. Along with the stresses of repeated heating and cooling cycles, grill burners face damage from salts and grease. Look for stainless steel here. A few manufacturers also offer heavy cast-brass burners, although the lead content of brass worries some grilling enthusiasts. On the plus side, brass can't rust, and the thick casting slows the rate at which the burners absorb and dissipate heat, contributing to longer life.

The newest trend in grill burners is infrared technology. A standard burner uses a series of small open flames to heat secondary elements, such as ceramic briquettes and metal cooking grates. An infrared burner concentrates the flame through a ceramic plate perforated with

◀ High-end performance and features aren't limited to built-in grills. This cart-mounted unit offers plenty of firepower and ample storage, with mobility.

thousands of microscopic holes. The process converts the fuel to infrared energy, which heats objects rather than the surrounding air. The result is a much more intense and concentrated heat that reaches temperatures of more than 1,000°F. By contrast, most convection-type grill burners peak at 600°F–750°F. Steak lovers swear by infrared cooking; for years restaurants have used it to sear flavors into premium cuts of meat. An added benefit is the reduction of flare-ups—the high heat vaporizes grease and oil instantly, so drippings from meat don't collect and provide fuel for open flames. This new cooking technology comes with a price tag twice as high as standard burners, however, and does have one drawback: the temperature range is too high for cooking some foods. A convection burner can maintain temperatures as low as 200°F. Combining infrared and standard burners in one unit makes a great package for outdoor grilling.

Cooking grates have traditionally been made of cast iron or chrome-plated steel, but those materials present problems of corrosion and sticking. Porcelain coatings have recently became commonplace on higher-quality grills; stainless steel and hard-anodized aluminum also offer great performance and easy cleaning.

Capacities and costs

High-end grills offer more bells and whistles features, such as better flame control, more reliable ignitions, accurate temperature gauges, and electronic meat probes. Most also have secondary cooking grates, which provide an additional shelf away from the burner to keep food warm or for cooking at a slower rate. With pricier grills, you also get size. A typical portable grill might offer 350 to 400 square inches of cooking surface and about 20,000 Btus (British thermal units, a measure of heat energy) of cooking power. It's not uncommon for built-in models to provide cooking areas of 600 to 1,000 square inches and a combined burner capacity of 60,000 Btus or more.

Quality comes at a price, and you'll see a wide range. A grill to be installed in a permanent outdoor kitchen ought to reflect the commitment you're making to the entire project. Why spend thousands of dollars on structures and landscaping only to cap it off with a $200 grill? If a portable grill makes the most sense for your backyard entertaining, make that choice, but premium cooking performance and durability won't start to appear on grills until you get above the $750 mark. For built-in grills, expect to spend at least $1,000 on an entry-level model. Most of the better-quality units will land somewhere in the range of $2,000 to $3,000. Splurge on a 60-inch stainless-steel grill with an integral side burner and rotisserie and you'll likely be writing a check for at least $5,000.

Accessories

Meals aren't just about what you can grill over an open flame. Many grill manufacturers offer side burners for cooking vegetables or other side dishes. Some include high-powered wok burners for stir-fry cooking or wok grates that you can substitute for the standard burner grate. If capacity and convenience are the reasons you want an outdoor kitchen, include at least one side burner in your design. Another feature that adds function to an outdoor kitchen is a rotisserie, which can be offered as an integral or a detachable unit.

Adequate storage is a must for a successful outdoor kitchen design. Many higher-end grills feature cart-mounted cabinets and shelves. Grill manufacturers also sell stainless-steel enclosures and access doors that you can install in a site-built cooking center. Check the resource guide in the back of the book for more information.

▶ An accurate temperature gauge allows you to better control the cooking process. Some grill models include a thermometer on the hood.

WORKING WITH CONTRACTORS

Most outdoor kitchen projects are within the reach of a seasoned do-it-yourselfer. If you want to hire the work out, you can find building trade professionals with the skills and experience to complete the job. Or you can combine some sweat equity with selective help from a few specialty contractors. In any case, start with an accurate assessment of your own abilities. Take inventory of the tasks you might want to tackle yourself. Add to that a clear idea of the contributions that professionals can make to your project.

Most of the labor involved in the typical outdoor kitchen project can be accomplished with tools that a homeowner might already have or can rent or purchase at a reasonable cost. (The exception is site excavation, which might require a backhoe or other heavy equipment.) Consider those tool costs. Estimate your time, both for doing work you know well and for learning new skills. Consider your physical health going into the project. Add up all those factors in deciding how much, if any, of the project you plan to tackle.

Getting professional help

There is one area where hiring a professional almost always pays off – project design. A licensed general architect or landscape architect or an independent residential designer can contribute in many ways to the success of a project. It's not just about having a great-looking kitchen, although that's certainly a goal. A design professional will bring familiarity with appropriate products and will understand the key technical issues that surface as a plan evolves. Whatever level of hands-on involvement you choose, make use of some of that expertise. There's nothing worse than spending a lot of time and money on a project and realizing you missed opportunities for a better or more functional design, and it may mean you'll recoup less of the investment later if potential home buyers spot the shortcomings.

■ **Do it all yourself.** Take the long view, and don't worry if you can't finish the project overnight. Work in phases to install a masonry wall, pour a new patio slab, build the cooking center, and so on. Pacing yourself this way might mean that an outdoor kitchen project begun this spring might not be enjoyed until next summer, but settling for incremental progress is easier on your body and budget.

■ **Be a construction manager.** Take care of getting the design sorted out and compiling a materials list and a project budget. In effect, you'll be acting as your own general contractor. You'll have to apply for the building permit and arrange inspections. You'll have to line up the subcontractors, brief them on the overall plan, then coordinate the scheduling to get them working on their contributions when the time comes. Comprehensive planning will make this easier, but the reliability of the independent subcontractors will be a big factor in how smoothly everything goes. And as a one-time residential customer, you're at a disadvantage compared to a bona fide general contractor who can dangle the carrot of future work in front of these tradespeople. Realize that you won't be a priority, but get firm commitments for start and finish dates nonetheless.

■ **Do the grunt work.** Building projects always involve some time-consuming, low-skill tasks. These can range from moving materials or picking up supplies to painting or routine job site cleanup. Some contractors have entry-level workers for these jobs, but if not they have to charge their going rate for simple tasks you might be able to do yourself. It may not be glamorous, but it can easily trim 20 percent or more from the project cost. Keep in mind, though, that you have to coordinate your work with that of the pros you hire, and you need to make the arrangements beforehand; some contractors prohibit homeowner help because of the liability risk.

■ **Cherry pick the work you want.** Some folks just like to build decks or plant flowers, even when they can pay someone else to do it for them. If there are certain tasks you really enjoy, or that you'd rather do than pay the pricey fees a specialist would charge, go for it. It might be the fun stuff, or just wrapping up finishing details when a professional has already paved the way by doing the more difficult part, such as rough plumbing or electrical work. You can install the faucet and prep sink once the supply and drain lines are roughed in, or wire receptacles after the conduit and cable have been installed.

■ **Enjoy watching from the sidelines.** Plenty of homeowners are happy to leave the sweating and fretting to contractors and their work crews. If the enjoyment of your outdoor kitchen doesn't have to include literally building it, limit yourself to monitoring the progress and writing the checks to pay for it all. This option is not for the faint of budget, however. In most building projects, materials and supply costs account for as little as one-fourth to one-third of the total budget. The rest is labor, overhead, and profit, and paying those expenses means your building dollars won't go nearly as far as if you pitched in. But going this route does mean that your contractor handles the project management chores for you. Contractors who specialize in outdoor kitchens are becoming increasingly common, which means they will bring fewer delays and costs surprises to most projects.

What to provide and expect from your contractor

If you decide to hire all or most of your kitchen construction to a professional contractor, there's still some involvement required on your part.

BUILDING CODES

Virtually every residential building project is subject to legal codes that govern the design and function of structural and mechanical details. Licensed contractors typically take care of these issues for the client, but if you are a DIY builder, it's your job. Get acquainted with the local building officials that approve plans and sign off on inspections, which cover:

■ Size and location of structure.
■ Type and depth of foundation.
■ Rough plumbing/electrical work.
■ Structural framing and features.
■ Stairs, steps, windows, doors.
■ Sheathing for walls and roof.
■ Finish plumbing/electrical work.

It's in your best interest to anticipate the various stages in the process and be ready for them. Here's what you can do:

■ **Be ready to build.** To provide an accurate cost estimate and do even the most preliminary work, a contractor will have to know most of the details of the project, from overall size to the kind of countertop surfaces you want. If you haven't sorted those things out yet, hire a designer first so you have a workable and detailed plan for building.

■ **Line up your funding.** To get an idea what to budget for a given project, contact some builders in your area and have them show you prior work and the cost ranges involved. This is not the same as getting a detailed estimate for your plan, but it will give you a ballpark figure to let you know if your budget is realistic. If the project is complex, reputable contractors will want to prepare a detailed scope-of-work proposal, which you'll likely have to pay for. Expect free estimates only for very simple projects or from subcontractors who are handling only limited aspects of the job, such as electrical or plumbing work. Any proposal should include itemized costs for labor and materials.

■ **Ask about different contract types.** Most builders work with a fixed bid contract because clients want to know the costs up front, and many include a margin to allow for unforeseen problems or delays. You end up paying that premium even if the job goes like clockwork. If you'd rather know exactly where your money is

going, ask about a cost plus contract. This involves straight billing for time and materials, and sometimes a markup for overhead and profit. Beware of open-ended contracts, though; the builder should still provide a completion date and a cost cap ahead of time.

■ **Discuss the procedure for change orders.** Revisions in even the best-laid plans are the rule in construction projects. Changes may increase or reduce costs, but regardless they should be documented in writing so everyone keeps similar expectations and clear goals.

■ **Negotiate a payment schedule in writing.** These will vary, depending on the size and complexity of a project. Smaller jobs will typically involve a 50 percent deposit upon a signed contract, with the remaining 50 percent due on completion. Many subcontractors will wait until completion for any payment, if their role is limited and the work quick. For larger projects, expect an incremental payment schedule that involves at least 30 percent down and two interim payments of 30 percent. The final 10 percent gets paid upon completion.

■ **Do your homework before you sign anything.** This means get references, look firsthand at previous work by the contractor, ask for a state license and proof of bond and insurance, and follow up to confirm that all are valid. This advice is so routine it's often overlooked, but it's often the most important thing you can do to ensure that a project gets completed successfully.

DESIGN GALLERY

Somewhere on the outdoor kitchen decision tree, between the Why of early daydreaming stages and the How of the hands-on construction work, there's an entire branch of What questions. As in "What exactly will my outdoor kitchen look like?" or "What features and amenities do I really want most?" And while each homeowner is likely to envision slightly different answers to those questions, there's something to be said for coveting your neighbor's kitchen ideas. This chapter is designed to let you do just that. You'll find dozens of great design elements, problem solving strategies, and creative layouts intended to address the very same design questions you're facing now. Originality, it's been said, is nothing but judicious imitation. That might be a bit harsh, especially when these outdoor kitchens offer so much inspiration.

FIESTA COLORS

Outdoor kitchens share certain basic functions, but their style possibilities range from rustic simplicity to cutting-edge contemporary. These projects show how versatile and imaginative the results can be. Mix colors, textures, and scale to create exactly the look you want.

■ South-of-the-border brightness gives this kitchen an unmistakably festive personality. Saltillo pavers and glased decorative tile are handmade touches that add to the festive look. A roof covers this cooking center so that wood cabinetry, decorative baskets, and an indoor gas range perform outdoors.

FAMILY OASIS

■ Ledgestone veneer and a sand-color concrete countertop give this outdoor kitchen the flavor of midwestern Prairie-style architecture. The tiered countertop design keeps food messes out of sight and offers a great spot for casual dining or an alfresco buffet.

CLASSICAL GAS

Modern amenities can coexist peacefully with ancient design, as this elegant installation clearly demonstrates. Custom fabrication of the fluted columns, moldings, and trim demanded a high-end budget. Ornate detailing such as this warrants adequate protection from the elements; here a roof extension provides shelter.

■ The use of ceramic tile and polished stone (or substitutes that mimic the look convincingly) makes sense aesthetically and practically. The atmosphere suggests a luxurious Roman villa, and the surfaces are durable and easy to keep clean.

HIDEAWAY HAVEN

Not all outdoor kitchens have to be grandly conspicuous. This full-featured installation boasts a fireplace, grill, undercounter refrigerator, and plenty of counter space, but it's tucked discreetly under the staircase of an upper-level deck. No function is lost, and the deck still gets top billing.

■ Integrating this cooking center into the deck structure leaves more open room on the patio, and it provides some shelter. The area behind the grill is actually an outdoor sitting room, complete with electric heat.

HEAT IS ON

A gas- or charcoal-burning grill is the centerpiece for most outdoor kitchens, but this California home boasts an ancient relative—a wood-burning oven. Good site planning is essential for such features, so fuel storage, smoke drift, and other concerns should be addressed before the kitchen is built.

■ **Functional layout is important in a large oudoor kitchen such as this one. Here the main work zone houses the oven, built-in grill, and a prep area with a dining counter and fabric canopy. A second station (inset) is used for canning fresh fruits and vegetables.**

GRAND ISLANDS

■ Tucked into a secluded corner of the patio, the cooking center (above) features a dining bar so guests can cheer the chef or sample goods hot off the grill.

The river-rock grilling station (below) offers the essentials of outdoor cooking—a grill, counter space, and a stable platform to stand on.

■ Fire and ice—a grill and refrigerator—balance the functional equation in this island cooking center (above, right). A simple L-shape kitchen (bottom, right) keeps a low profile against a canyon hillside.

UNDER COVER

■ Modular stainless-steel base cabinets make cleaning easier when you have to hose down the patio. The ceramic tile backsplash was applied over brick siding, so heat from the grill (inset) isn't a problem. A custom enclosure camouflages the vent hood.

A partially enclosed rear porch offers an ideal location for an outdoor kitchen with indoor features. This example takes advantage of its sheltered setting by incorporating cabinetry, wall-mounted display storage, a prep sink, and undercounter appliances into a user-friendly layout. There's even a wok burner next to the grill. If this kind of attached kitchen suits you, plan for a vent hood to exhaust the smoke and cooking fumes through the roof.

▲ A dining area, fireplace, and deck (above) share the same roof that covers the outdoor kitchen. Not only does the proximity add convenience, it creates the ambience of an indoor great room.

◀ The peninsula (left) adds storage and function to the kitchen area and offers seating for casual dining.

STAYING CONNECTED

These outdoor kitchens share a common virtue–a nearly seamless connection to their surroundings. Being tethered directly to the house helps, but more critical is a deliberate use of color, materials, and other elements that establish the connection between the home and its "siblings."

■ This poolside kitchen benefits from a sheltering roof and archways that let breezes meander through the dining area. The simple color scheme—warm yellow walls, white trim, and terra-cotta tile on the floor and countertops—keeps it serene.

▲ This compact kitchen (above) shows that good things do come in small packages. There's a prep sink, refrigerator, grill, and even a dining counter, all tucked under a cozy gazebo roof.

▼ A versatile kitchen "closet" (below, left) combines protection and convenience. A set of bifold doors keeps dust at bay when idle or conceals the mess until you get a chance to clean up.

▲ Tucking an outdoor kitchen along an exterior wall often ensures a seamless connection to the house, especially if the siding or finish is duplicated on the kitchen base. This house (above) has a hand-troweled stucco finish.

KITCHENS YOU CAN BUILD

Do you want to learn more about what it takes to create a great outdoor kitchen? This section takes you through 10 projects from across the country, each with its own mix of materials, features, and design strategies. Some have site considerations that called for particular structural solutions or materials, while others are designed around a group of core functional amenities. All reflect the owners' enthusiasm for fun and stylish outdoor living.

Because site conditions determine the design of an outdoor kitchen, don't insist on duplicating any of these projects exactly. Focus on the key features that appeal to you and adapt them to an installation that fits your yard and climate.

Each project includes commentary, photos, and illustrations that explain the basics of how the kitchen can be constructed. The details shown reflect proven techniques and materials that are friendly to do-it-yourselfers; most, however, can be built using alternate construction methods and materials. Be sure to check local building codes as you plan your outdoor kitchen.

PROJECT 1
CLASSIC BRICK COURTYARD

The timeless appeal of brick makes it a classic material for an outdoor kitchen. For this installation, sloped terrain complicates the structural requirements. The tall back wall extends beyond the cooking center and surrounds the rest of the courtyard. Concrete block offers a simple and affordable solution. Once you've poured a solid concrete footing along the site for the wall, the block goes up. Steel reinforcing rods and concrete fill turn the block wall into a solid structural unit.

You can face the wall with full brick, but applying a ½-inch-thick brick veneer is easier and faster. The concrete block supplies all the strength needed for the structure.

A similar approach works for the cooking center. Concrete block forms the core of the structure, which features a drop-in bay for the grill and two stainless-steel cabinet doors for access to storage space and the sink connections. Angle-iron lintels provide support for the facing and countertop over the access openings, and a reinforced plywood subbase provides the surface for the cement backer board and ceramic tile countertop. Thin brick veneer is applied as the decorative surface for the kitchen base.

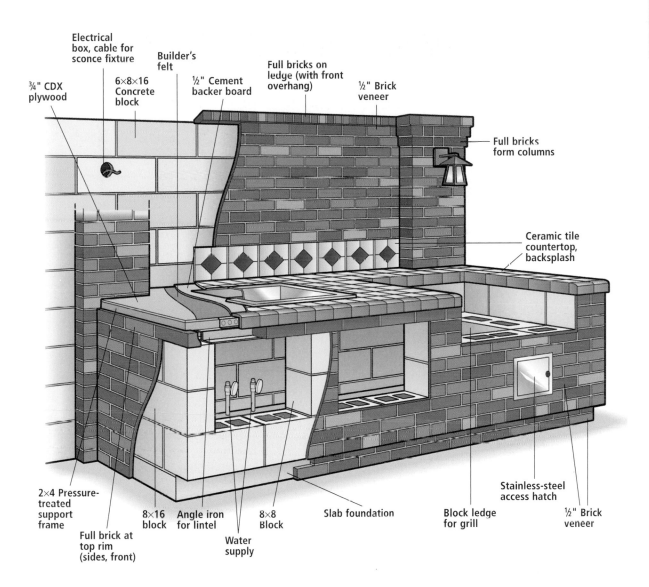

Electrical box, cable for sconce fixture

Builder's felt

Full bricks on ledge (with front overhang)

¾" CDX plywood

6×8×16 Concrete block

½" Cement backer board

½" Brick veneer

Full bricks form columns

Ceramic tile countertop, backsplash

2×4 Pressure-treated support frame

Full brick at top rim (sides, front)

8×16 block

Angle iron for lintel

Water supply

8×8 Block

Slab foundation

Block ledge for grill

Stainless-steel access hatch

½" Brick veneer

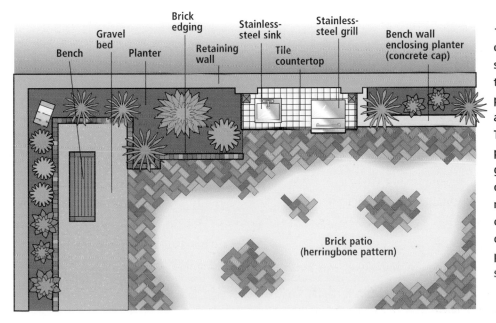

Bench

Gravel bed

Planter

Brick edging

Retaining wall

Stainless-steel sink

Tile countertop

Stainless-steel grill

Bench wall enclosing planter (concrete cap)

Brick patio (herringbone pattern)

◄ If you prefer your outdoor kitchen to be a supporting actor instead of the star of the show, a perimeter installation such as this one makes sense. The rest of the landscape— plants, brick patio, the garden bench—has plenty of room to shine. Although not as convenient as a cooking center attached to or near the house, this project functions more as a separate environment.

Getting started

This outdoor kitchen is part of an expansive backyard setting that includes other features. The entire yard is surrounded by a masonry wall, which serves as both a privacy screen (along the sides of the yard) and a retaining wall (along the rear of the yard, where the cooking center is located).

The wall has to withstand some lateral force from the slope behind it, mostly at the base. Concrete and block provide an alternative to all-brick-and-mortar construction and allow for a slimmer profile. When surfaced with brick veneer, the concrete structure can still provide the traditional look. A specialty contractor could form and pour solid concrete walls, but block construction is less expensive, especially if you do the work yourself (see page 126).

Because of the brick detailing that will come later, it's better to use 6-inch-wide block for the wall rather than the more common 8-inch block. The narrower block allows for a front overhang when standard 8-inch-long brick is used for the cap course on the wall. If your site features a steep slope that will add pressure on the retaining wall, consult an engineer or a building official about using 8-inch or wider block. If you must use wider block, you'll also have to use oversize brick to cap the wall.

Start with a poured concrete footing about 10 inches thick and 16 inches wide (above right). Before pouring the concrete, add lengths of steel reinforcing rod inside the footing and run electrical conduit for the two light fixtures that flank the cooking center. When the footing has cured a week and the forms have been stripped, backfill the outer side with crushed rock and install drainpipe (opposite below). Then lay and mortar the block in place.

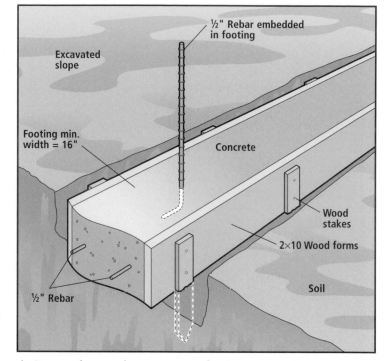

▲ Form and pour a heavy concrete footing to provide a secure base for the retaining wall. Taller walls and/or steep slopes will require a thicker and wider footing to provide necessary ballast.

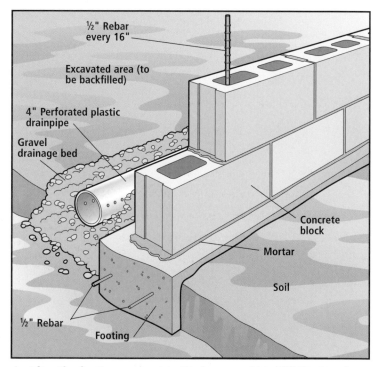

▲ After the footing cures, strip the forms and backfill the trench with crushed rock for drainage. Include a perforated drainpipe to divert water away from the wall. Mortar the block in place, then fill the hollows with concrete.

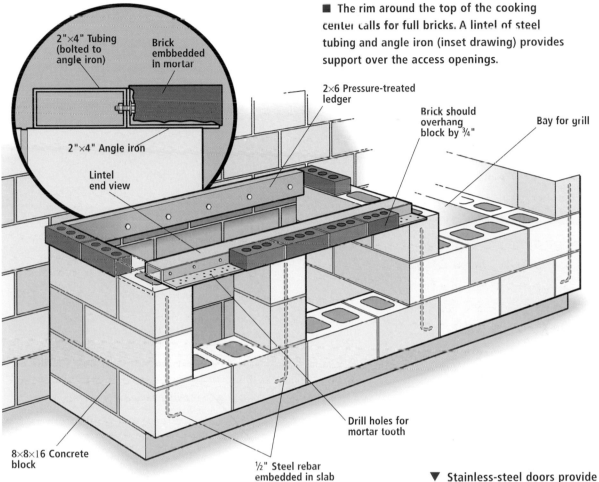

■ The rim around the top of the cooking center calls for full bricks. A lintel of steel tubing and angle iron (inset drawing) provides support over the access openings.

2"×4" Tubing (bolted to angle iron)

Brick embbedded in mortar

2"×4" Angle iron

Lintel end view

2×6 Pressure-treated ledger

Brick should overhang block by ¾"

Bay for grill

Drill holes for mortar tooth

8×8×16 Concrete block

½" Steel rebar embedded in slab

Building the cooking center

The cooking center also needs a foundation, which can take the form of a perimeter footing like the wall or a concrete slab as shown. Run electrical conduit, gas line, or plumbing lines before pouring the slab (see page 154). The block construction is similar to that used for the wall, but the access openings and the narrow band of brick above them require special construction technique. Concrete block is too tall to create the narrow top course above the access bays. Instead install an angle-iron lintel and a row of full standard bricks. Set the bricks with their faces overhanging ¾ inch from the block below so that when the brick veneer is

▼ Stainless-steel doors provide access to plumbing and storage.

■ Accessory features such as the stainless-steel access doors must be fastened to the masonry substrate. Drill holes for expansion anchors and tap the anchors in place. Then fit the metal frame and secure with stainless-steel sheet metal screws.

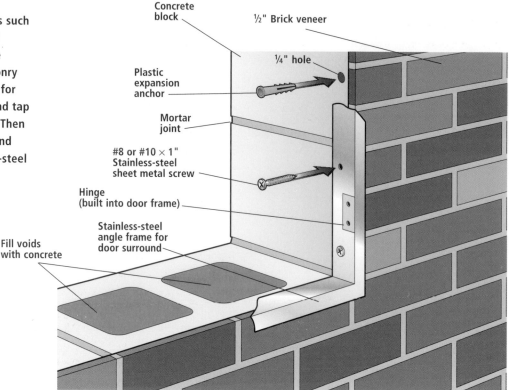

Concrete block

½" Brick veneer

¼" hole

Plastic expansion anchor

Mortar joint

#8 or #10 × 1" Stainless-steel sheet metal screw

Hinge (built into door frame)

Stainless-steel angle frame for door surround

Fill voids with concrete

installed, the surfaces will be flush. To keep the brick veneer courses consistent, work down from the top row.

As an alternative you can substitute full brick for the concrete block and veneer combination, though it will likely take longer to build the cooking center base.

Take care to align the top edges of all the bricks or blocks in the top course to create a flat base for the countertop. Use pressure-treated lumber and ¾-inch exterior plywood to create a stout frame and substrate assembly for the countertop (see construction view illustration on page 53). Fasten cement backer board to the plywood and use thinset mortar to set the tile.

Installing fixtures and access doors

The cooking center base includes ledges to support the grill. With masonry construction and a ceramic tile countertop, no insulating liner is needed for fireproofing. (The grill manufacturer may include a steel insulating liner that can be used.) Set the grill in place and connect the gas line or propane tank.

Test-fit the metal door frames for the access bays, then use masonry anchors and screws to secure them. Fit the doors per the manufacturer's instructions and adjust their clearances before you tighten all the frame screws. If you include a sink, fit it into the countertop and make the necessary water supply and drain connections.

Project sequence

Here are the basic steps involved in building this kitchen. Remember to check with your local building officials about required inspections.

- Excavate and grade for wall footing and patio.
- Set footing forms; add rebar; pour concrete.
- Lay concrete block for retaining wall.
- Add gravel backfill and drainpipe behind wall.
- Set forms and underground utilities for slab.
- Pour slab for cooking center; add block walls.
- Construct planter footings and block walls.
- Fill all hollow block bays with concrete.
- Install angle iron lintels; cap with mortar and full brick to create "rim" of cooking center.
- Apply brick veneer to visible wall surfaces.
- Use full bricks for columns and cap on wall.
- Build wood substrate for countertop base.
- Install backer board and tile on countertop.
- Fit grill, sink, accessories; complete hookups.
- Compact crushed rock bed for patio base.
- Spread and screed sand for brick base.
- Install brick pavers; add sand to joints.

ESSENTIALS

PRIMARY SKILLS REQUIRED:

FORMING AND POURING A CONCRETE FOOTING; BUILDING A CONCRETE BLOCK WALL; FORMING AND POURING A CONCRETE SLAB; LAYING BRICK; INSTALLING BRICK VENEER; BASIC PLUMBING AND ELECTRICAL SKILLS; INSTALLING CERAMIC TILE.

TOOLS TO RENT OR OWN:

WATER LEVEL OR TRANSIT; PORTABLE CIRCULAR SAW; WET-CUTTING MASONRY SAW; CONCRETE-FINISHING TOOLS; TILE SAW; VIBRATING COMPACTOR FOR PATIO BASE.

MATERIALS YOU'LL NEED:

FORM LUMBER; READY-MIX CONCRETE; 6-INCH-WIDE CONCRETE BLOCK; STANDARD CLAY BRICK (NEW OR USED); MATCHING BRICK VENEER (½ INCH THICK); 2×4 FRAMING LUMBER AND PLYWOOD SHEATHING FOR COUNTERTOP BASE; CEMENT BACKER BOARD; BRICK PAVERS, GRAVEL, AND SAND FOR PATIO BASE.

◀ Extensive hardscaping and a variety of plants garner the most attention in this courtyard. The cooking center (on the right), while large and well-equipped, doesn't dominate the space but stands ready for use.

PROJECT 2
UNDER THE BIG TOP

Although brick, stone, and other masonry materials are natural choices for outdoor use, there are many other options to choose. This outdoor kitchen shows that wood can do the job nicely as long as it gets some shelter from the elements. In this case protection comes in the form of a fabric roof. Made of an awning-like material designed for continuous outdoor use, the tent keeps the rain and the harshest sun at bay, so only cold winter temperatures have enough clout to drive the family indoors. The roof is supported by a framework of wood rafters and four laminated arches rising gracefully from the deck floor.

The arches were designed by an architect and custom-made. They added to the cost of the project, but the investment offers some payback: Protection from the weather allows the use of wood for the deck and cooking center—a material that is less expensive and easier to build with than concrete, block, brick, and tile. The translucent quality of the cover helps maintain a true outdoor feeling in the space, something that might have been lost with a conventional sheathing-and-shingle roof.

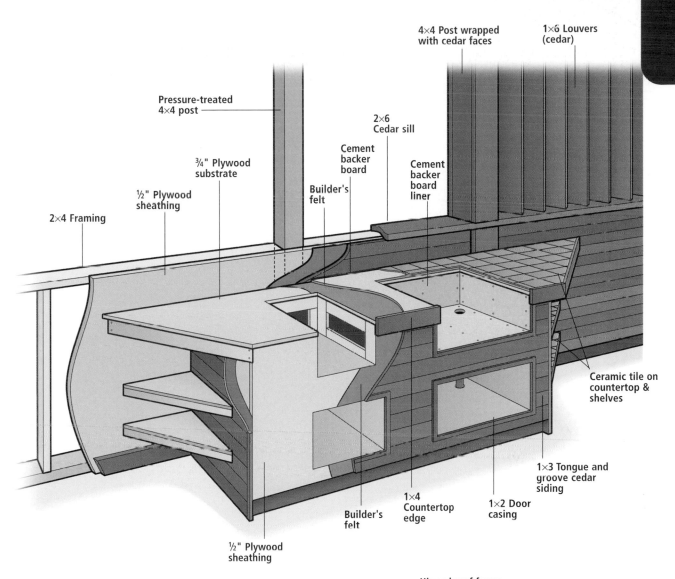

4×4 Post wrapped with cedar faces

1×6 Louvers (cedar)

Pressure-treated 4×4 post

2×6 Cedar sill

¾" Plywood substrate

Cement backer board

Cement backer board liner

½" Plywood sheathing

Builder's felt

2×4 Framing

Ceramic tile on countertop & shelves

1×3 Tongue and groove cedar siding

Builder's felt

1×4 Countertop edge

1×2 Door casing

½" Plywood sheathing

■ Even though it's shielded by the roof and a louvered wall, the cooking center will need sealants, hardware, and finishes rated for outdoor applications. In addition, the use of wood does raise the issue of combustibility. With a gas grill and burner unit, the wood frame structure will need insulating materials to ensure safety. As shown here, each bay is lined with cement backer board, a masonry product used for tile installation. Some grill manufacturers provide insulated metal liners that accomplish the same thing.

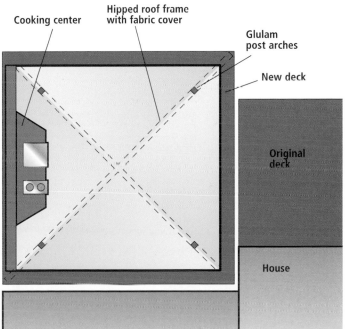

Cooking center

Hipped roof frame with fabric cover

Glulam post arches

New deck

Original deck

House

▶ Perched at the edge of a newly constructed deck, this wall incorporates materials and methods similar to any exterior wall. Plywood sheathing covers pressure-treated framing lumber; then a layer of builder's felt and lap siding finish the look. Angled louvers on the top half deflect any strong winds but offer plenty of ventilation.

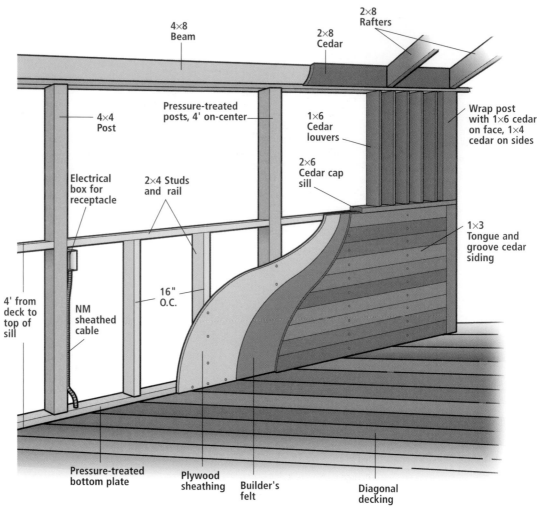

2×8 Rafters

4×8 Beam

2×8 Cedar

4×4 Post

Pressure-treated posts, 4' on-center

1×6 Cedar louvers

Wrap post with 1×6 cedar on face, 1×4 cedar on sides

Electrical box for receptacle

2×4 Studs and rail

2×6 Cedar cap sill

1×3 Tongue and groove cedar siding

4' from deck to top of sill

NM sheathed cable

16" O.C.

Pressure-treated bottom plate

Plywood sheathing

Builder's felt

Diagonal decking

Getting started

This project might seem ambitious, but except for the custom arches, most of the work requires only basic carpentry skills. What's more, you can tackle the work in phases to keep it manageable. Start with the platform deck, which is where everything connects. The how-to section on deck construction (see page 144) outlines the basic tools and techniques, but this project requires a few twists.

First consider the site factors, a preliminary step that applies to any deck. In this project the large square footprint drives the design more deliberately than smaller decks or decks that must follow the terrain more closely. The tent

top fits naturally over a square frame; however, an awning shop—which will have to make the fabric cover—can advise you about other options for the overall shape.

More critical is the foundation work for supporting the four corner posts and arches, which carry most of the weight of the roof. Standard concrete piers can support the deck's floor beams, but you'll need four oversize piers directly under the arch posts. Anchor the posts to the deck beams and floor with heavy steel hardware. Consult an architect to help design the post layout and the foundation piers, and be sure to check applicable building codes.

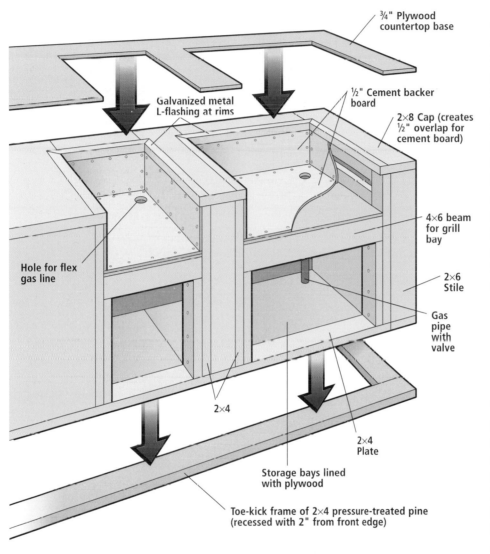

¾" Plywood countertop base

Galvanized metal L-flashing at rims

½" Cement backer board

2×8 Cap (creates ½" overlap for cement board)

4×6 beam for grill bay

2×6 Stile

Gas pipe with valve

Hole for flex gas line

2×4

2×4 Plate

Storage bays lined with plywood

Toe-kick frame of 2×4 pressure-treated pine (recessed with 2" from front edge)

◄ Simple 2x framing, wrapped with exterior plywood sheathing, provides the structural base for the grill cabinet. Cement backer board (capped with galvanized metal flashing) lines the bays for the grill and side burner. This version gets a ceramic tile countertop and tongue-and-groove siding, but once the basic structure is built, you can finish it with other materials if you wish.

▼ Fire hazards are always a concern when high-heat appliances are used near combustible materials. Most manufacturers of built-in grills and side burners offer a metal insulating liner if you request it.

The wall behind the cooking center also supports some of the roof weight. To handle that load, install 4×4 posts and a 4×8 beam to form the basic structure. Conventional stud wall framing (see page 150) fills each section and provides a nailing base for the sheathing and siding. Fit the top half of the wall with 1×6 cedar louvers installed with gaps for ventilation.

Building the cooking center

Because the cooking center cabinet supports the weight of the grill and the burner unit, it calls

Trim pieces fit
around rafters

Glulam beam

Translucent, waterproof
roof material

▲ The hipped roof, with its four
triangular faces, is more challenging
to build than a simple gable roof, but
a rafter guide will explain the
geometry required. Detailing and trim
improve the appearance of the frame.

for a stout framework you won't find in typical
interior kitchen cabinetry (illustration page 61).
Using pressure-treated lumber for the frame
safeguards the structure against insect and
moisture damage. Treat the exterior finish
surfaces as you would any outside structure,
using weather-resistant materials and applying
appropriate coatings or sealants.

For the tile countertops and shelves, choose a
vitreous ceramic tile (see page 143). Although
the kitchen is protected from rain, regular soap-
and-water cleanup sessions will be necessary.

The roof structure

The addition of a roof is certainly a practical
choice for this kitchen, but the graceful look
provided by the translucent fabric and the
arches also gives it a signature style. They do
add some complexity, however, and most folks

GLULAM BASICS

Engineered-wood building materials may be
mistaken by some as second-rate substitutes
for solid timbers. In fact, these products often do
what sawn lumber can't—the glulam arches in
this project prove the point. Short for "glued and
laminated timber," glulams are built from multiple
layers of thinner boards glued together with
powerful adhesives. They can take on graceful
shapes or handle long spans without support.
Special equipment is required to produce them.
Aside from a few standard post and beam sizes,
they are often made-to-order for a building.

◀ The covered deck provides protection from sun and snow while offering unobstructed views of prairie and mountain landscapes.

will want to recruit the help of a professional for this part of the project.

For starters, the arch posts are custom-made laminated timbers called glulams and are not a do-it-yourself project. (For more about glulam timbers, see the opposite page.)

In addition, roof framing is more involved than building floors and walls. Along with the geometry of laying out the roof, you face the added difficulty of lifting and working above your head. A good framing guide (with rise-and-run calculations and span tables for rafters) is essential. This is one phase of the project worth hiring out.

ESSENTIALS

PRIMARY SKILLS REQUIRED:

MEASURING AND LAYOUT; FORMING AND POURING CONCRETE FOOTINGS; BASIC DECK AND WALL FRAMING; BASIC ELECTRICAL AND PLUMBING SKILLS; GENERAL WOODWORKING; ROOF FRAMING (IF NOT SUBCONTRACTED).

TOOLS TO OWN OR RENT:

WATER LEVEL OR BUILDER'S TRANSIT; POWER POSTHOLE AUGER; WHEELBARROW; CORDLESS DRILL/DRIVER; PORTABLE CIRCULAR SAW; TABLE SAW; BASIC CARPENTRY TOOLS; PIPE WRENCH; TILE CUTTER.

MATERIALS YOU'LL NEED:

READY-MIX CONCRETE; PRESSURE-TREATED FRAMING LUMBER; WOOD OR COMPOSITE DECKING; ELECTRICAL CONDUIT AND CABLE; PLUMBING SUPPLIES; PLYWOOD SHEATHING; GLULAM POSTS OR SUBSTITUTE; CEDAR LUMBER FOR ROOF AND TRIM; CEDAR TONGUE-AND-GROOVE SIDING; PAINTS OR SEALERS; CEMENT BACKER BOARD; SEMIVITREOUS OR VITREOUS CERAMIC TILE.

Project sequence

With a multidimensional project such as this, it's important to have the entire plan sorted out before you begin. The building process can be approached in a series of manageable steps:

■ Measure the site and mark the pier locations.
■ Dig holes for the concrete piers, including the four oversize footings to support the roof posts.
■ Pour concrete footings/piers.
■ Build deck frame of posts, beams, joists.
■ Run electrical conduit and gas lines as needed.
■ Install decking material.
■ Frame and sheathe wall that backs cooking area.
■ Secure post base hardware to deck.
■ Erect arch posts (glulam or other) at corners.
■ Complete roof frame with rafters and fascia.
■ Add roof trim and moldings.
■ Paint or seal wood surfaces as desired.
■ Attach fabric roof cover (hire a professional installer).
■ Build base cabinet for cooking center.
■ Add siding or finish materials to wall, cabinet.
■ Build doors for cooking center cabinet.
■ Paint or seal finish woodwork as desired.
■ Install countertop substrate/triangle shelves.
■ Install ceramic tile on countertops and shelves.
■ Install gas grill and side burner unit.

PROJECT 3
ROCK SOLID

This kitchen is part of an entire outdoor environment, complete with a landscape retaining wall, curved planters with built-in benches, a large brick patio, and even an outdoor fireplace with a towering chimney. The homeowners were fortunate enough to live near an old riverbed quarry, which provided all the stone required. Most people don't have their own neighborhood quarry, but that's no reason to give up a look like this. These plans call for a simple approach. Inexpensive concrete block, reinforced with steel rebar and a poured concrete fill, provides the structure, which was overlaid with manufactured stone veneer. Manufactured stone costs about the same as most natural stone, but the light weight, uniform quality, and prefabricated corner units make installation quicker and easier. It's also less costly to ship and offers a wider variety of styles and colors than any natural stone you are likely to find in any one region. The brick patio floor is just the right accent, adding rich texture and color. The bench caps for the planter walls are poured on-site using simple forms made of plywood and 2× lumber and then set in place.

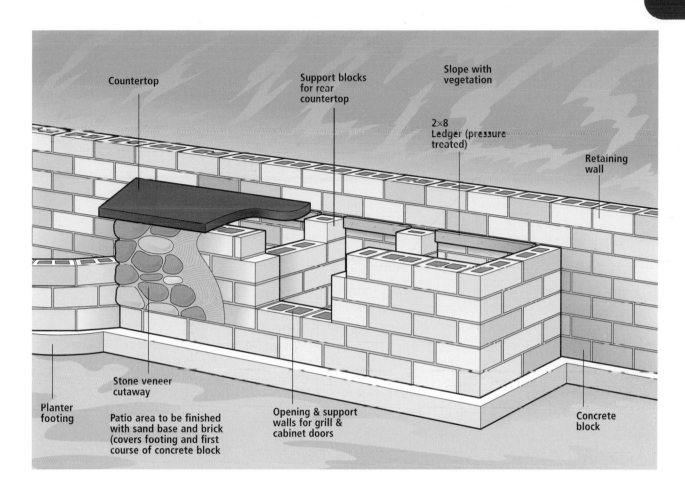

Countertop

Support blocks
for rear
countertop

Slope with
vegetation

2×8
Ledger (pressure
treated)

Retaining
wall

Stone veneer
cutaway

Planter
footing

Patio area to be finished
with sand base and brick
(covers footing and first
course of concrete block

Opening & support
walls for grill &
cabinet doors

Concrete
block

■ This cutaway construction view (above) reveals the basic anatomy of the cooking center. A concrete slab provides the footing, supporting five courses of 8-inch-tall block. Inside, two partitions create a ledge to support the grill. A site-built concrete countertop with angled ends caps it off. The floor plan (right) reveals the flow across the patio area.

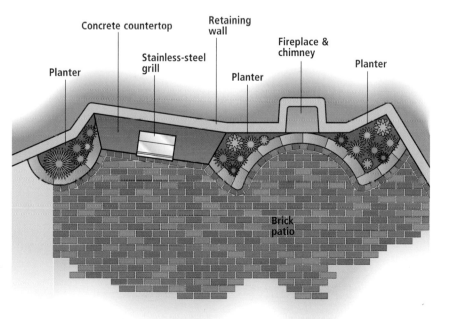

Concrete countertop

Retaining
wall

Fireplace &
chimney

Planter

Stainless-steel
grill

Planter

Planter

Planter

Brick
patio

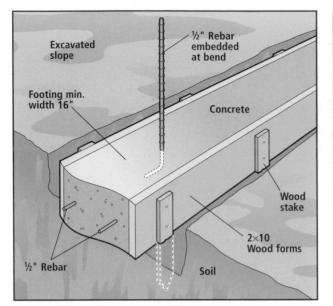

▲ A poured concrete footing, reinforced with steel rebar, is required to support the retaining wall. The longer the concrete cures, the stronger it will be, so leave the forms on for several days to help keep the concrete damp.

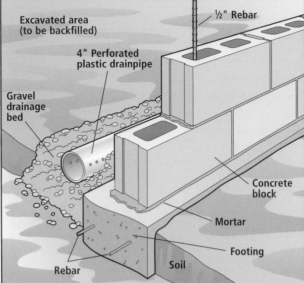

▲ After the footing cures, the block wall is mortared in place. Lay perforated plastic drainpipe in a drainage bed of crushed rock to transport water away and reduce the soil pressure against the back of the wall.

Getting started

If you plan to have a concrete wall (either block or poured) as part of your outdoor landscape, your first step will be to pour a footing (see page 127). Typically the footing should be at least twice as wide as the width of the wall and about 8 to 10 inches thick. It should be even larger for retaining walls. (Check with your local building official for specific requirements.)

Horizontal lengths of steel reinforcing rod (rebar) ½ inch in diameter will help the footing resist cracking and shifting. Set a few lengths of rebar vertically into the footing when it's poured (illustration above left). Space the rebar every 16 inches for walls more than 4 feet tall, and about every 4 feet for shorter walls. Place bars so they run through the hollow cavities in the blocks. After all the walls are built, you'll fill the cavities with concrete, creating a solid reinforced wall. If scheduling allows, let the

footing cure at least a week before stripping the forms and building the walls.

Retaining walls have to withstand tremendous pressure from the weight of the soil, especially when it's wet. To relieve some of this pressure, provide drainage for the excess water that would otherwise stay trapped behind the wall. A bed of crushed rock along the footing and a run of perforated drainpipe will do the trick. Lay the pipe with its perforation holes on the sides (see illustration above right).

Any adjoining structure, such as the planter, will also need a footing, but for the cooking center a standard 4-inch-thick slab will provide an adequate foundation. Place the underground conduit or gas lines before pouring the slab (see page 154). Because the block wall and other structures in this project will be covered with stone veneer, you don't need to tool the mortar joints in the wall or other structures. Just clear

▶ As the connecting walls go up, tether them to the retaining wall. Use a small hammer and chisel or piece of rebar to punch small holes in several blocks; then as you construct the wall, mortar in several short Z-bend lengths of rebar to tie the sections together. The wood ledger for supporting the countertop has been attached using anchors and screws; the gas line and valve were installed before the slab was poured.

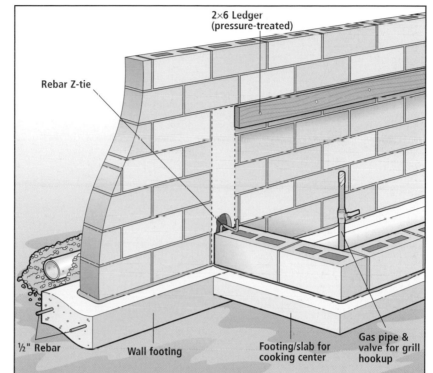

2×6 Ledger (pressure-treated)

Rebar Z-tie

½" Rebar

Wall footing

Footing/slab for cooking center

Gas pipe & valve for grill hookup

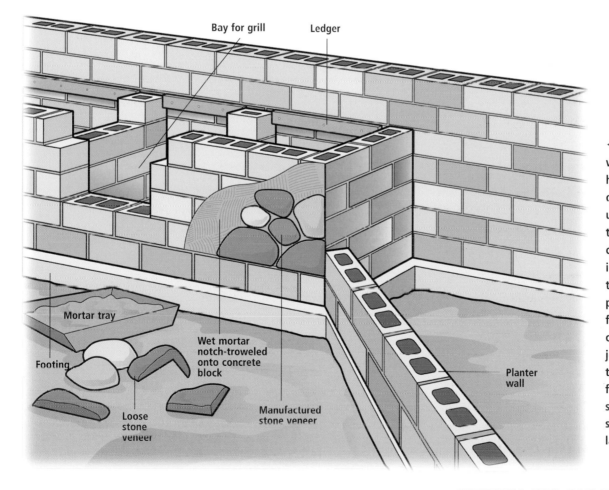

Bay for grill

Ledger

Mortar tray

Footing

Loose stone veneer

Wet mortar notch-troweled onto concrete block

Manufactured stone veneer

Planter wall

◀ In climates where frost heaving might occur or on unstable soil, the planter walls can "float" independently of the others by pouring separate footings and caulking the joints between the walls. To finish the structures, apply stone veneer in a layer of mortar.

■ An outdoor fireplace requires special materials, including firebrick for the box lining (installed with heat-tolerant refractory mortar) and flue inserts for the chimney. A skilled mason should build it.

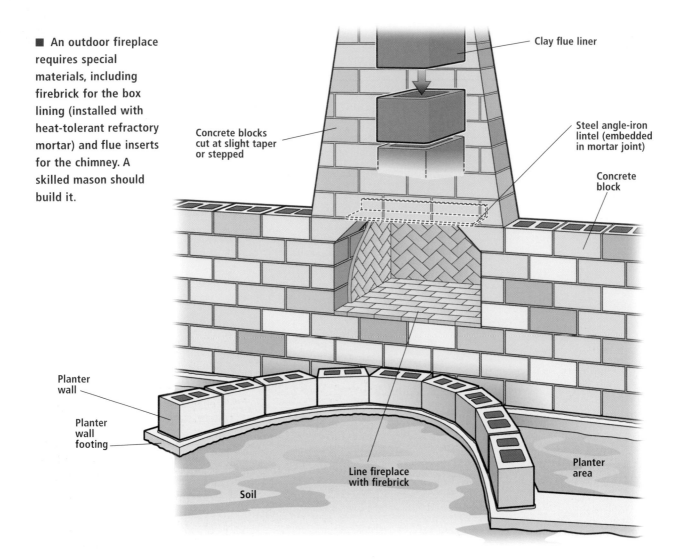

Clay flue liner

Concrete blocks cut at slight taper or stepped

Steel angle-iron lintel (embedded in mortar joint)

Concrete block

Planter wall

Planter wall footing

Line fireplace with firebrick

Planter area

Soil

any excess mortar off the surface with a flat trowel as you work. Access doors or other hardware should be installed before applying the stone veneer.

Fireplace option

Outdoor fireplaces add atmosphere to any patio or landscape design. If you live in a city, though, expect legal hurdles. Because of increasingly strict air-quality standards, in many areas the use of outdoor fireplaces has been curtailed or banned altogether. Get legal approval before proceeding with this feature.

If you get approval for a fireplace, recruit a professional mason or experienced contractor to build it. Whether it's a prefab metal modular system or a site-built masonry unit, a fireplace demands specialized knowledge and materials to ensure safety and performance.

Finishing touches

The cooking center and fireplace are obviously the highlights of this installation, but this project's appeal extends beyond the hearth areas. The graceful contours of the planter beds and the plants themselves soften the imposing presence of the structures. The planters are easy to build. As with the wall and cooking center, start with a level footing. Lay the block courses for the planter walls. The stone veneer hides the block work. Cap the planter walls with concrete bench sections, formed and poured on-site (below, left).

Project sequence

With a design as elaborate as this, there are plenty of details you might have to adapt to your own site, but you can still plan according to a basic construction sequence:

- Set perimeter stakes to define project area.
- Excavate and grade for wall footing, slab.
- Set forms; add rebar.
- Lay concrete block for retaining wall.
- Add drainpipe behind wall; backfill.
- Set forms and underground utilities for slabs
- Pour and finish slabs for cooking center and adjoining structures.

- Build block walls for cooking center.
- Build block structure for fireplace/chimney.
- Line firebox and flue with required materials.
- Construct planter footings and block walls.
- Fill hollow block bays with concrete.
- Apply stone veneer to visible wall surfaces.
- Form and pour colored concrete countertop.
- Compact crushed rock bed for patio base.
- Spread and screed sand for brick base.
- Install brick pavers on patio; add sand to paver joints.
- Install grill; complete any utility hookups.

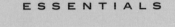

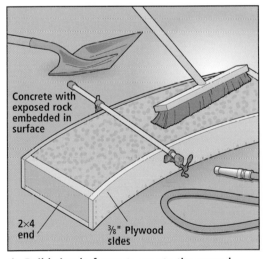

▲ Build simple forms to create the curved concrete seats for the planter walls. Fasten ³⁄₈-inch plywood sides to a plywood bottom cut to the desired contours; use 2×4 stock for the ends. Fill the form about halfway with concrete, add wire reinforcing mesh, then pour the rest of the concrete. For an exposed-aggregate finish, use a float to embed a layer of small pebbles, wait until concrete sets, then brush with a broom and hose the surface.

Concrete with exposed rock embedded in surface
2×4 end
³⁄₈" Plywood sides

ESSENTIALS

PRIMARY SKILLS REQUIRED:
FORMING AND POURING A CONCRETE WALL FOOTING AND A CONCRETE SLAB; LAYING BLOCK; MORTARING STONE VENEER.

TOOLS TO OWN OR RENT:
WATER LEVEL OR TRANSIT; WET-CUTTING MASONRY SAW; CONCRETE FINISHING TOOLS.

MATERIALS YOU'LL NEED:
FORM LUMBER; SAND; GRAVEL; READY-MIX CONCRETE; CONCRETE BLOCK; REBAR; MORTAR; MANUFACTURED STONE VENEER; BRICK PAVERS.

▼ The brick pavers on the patio need a stable substrate. Start with a layer of compacted crushed stone, then add a compacted sand bed (see page 123).

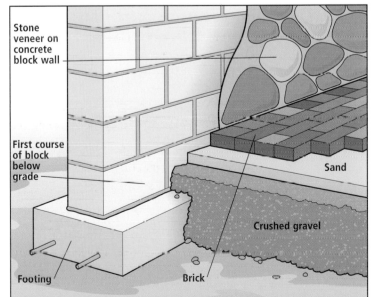

Stone veneer on concrete block wall
First course of block below grade
Footing
Brick
Sand
Crushed gravel

PROJECT 4
FIRE AND SHELTER

For some the idea of an outdoor kitchen conjures up images of the simple life. Forget the sink and the refrigerator, even the gas grill. These people don't mind the temporary loss of a few conveniences. If that fits your dreams of outdoor living, here's a project to consider. It consists of just two core elements: a simple dining shelter called a loggia and an in-ground pit for cooking over a wood fire. In addition, the landscaping contributes to the low-tech appeal of the area. Stone-wall planters double as benches around the fire pit—simple but not primitive.

The design choices use basic construction techniques as well. The loggia features a half-wall surround of concrete block finished with hand-troweled stucco. The wall is capped with red cedar sills, posts, beams, and lath that offer a sense of shelter without feeling closed in.

The homeowners originally developed the fire pit as a simple hole in the ground, in the style of a rustic cooking pit. When they later hired a landscape architect to redesign the outdoor space, they upgraded the pit to include a concrete surround lined with firebrick, a cedar hatch, and a custom-built rotisserie.

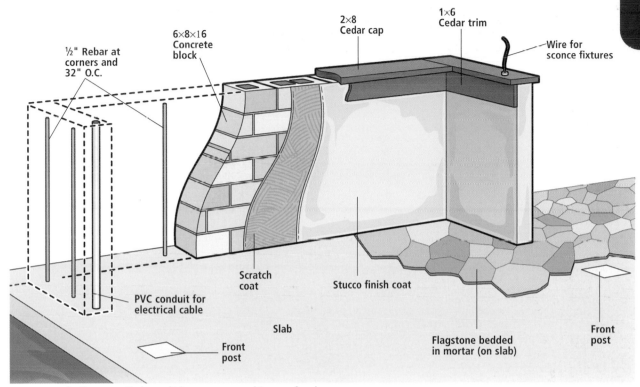

½" Rebar at corners and 32" O.C.

6×8×16 Concrete block

2×8 Cedar cap

1×6 Cedar trim

Wire for sconce fixtures

Scratch coat

Stucco finish coat

PVC conduit for electrical cable

Slab

Front post

Flagstone bedded in mortar (on slab)

Front post

▲ Because it doesn't house any cooking or food prep features, the loggia is simpler to build than most outdoor kitchen structures. The block wall has steel reinforcing bar embedded in the cavities, which are filled with concrete. Troweled stucco covers the block, and a cedar sill caps it.

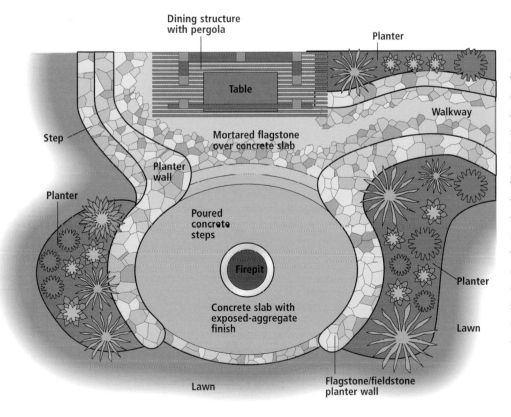

Dining structure with pergola

Planter

Table

Walkway

Step

Planter wall

Planter

Poured concrete steps

Mortared flagstone over concrete slab

Firepit

Planter

Concrete slab with exposed-aggregate finish

Lawn

Lawn

Flagstone/fieldstone planter wall

◄ Contrasting elements work together in this outdoor cooking and dining area. The rectangular shelter houses a table and benches, while a series of gracefully curved walls and walkways meanders through the site. Textures vary to create interest. The random edges of the flagstone walls and the ornate plantings are countered by simpler surfaces such as the exposed-aggregate patio and smooth stucco walls.

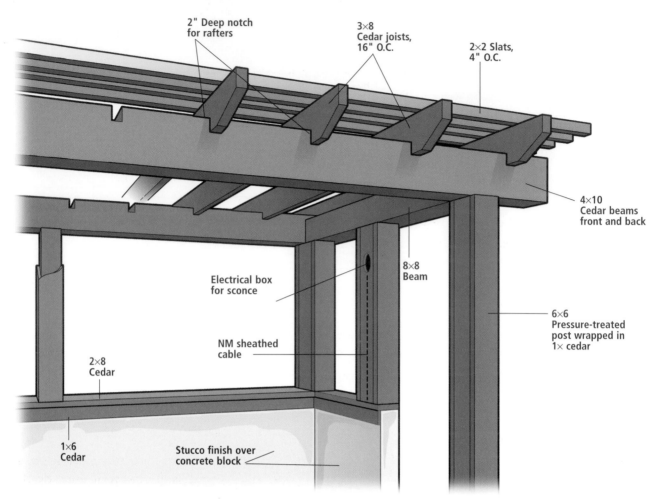

2" Deep notch
for rafters

3×8
Cedar joists,
16" O.C.

2×2 Slats,
4" O.C.

4×10
Cedar beams
front and back

8×8
Beam

Electrical box
for sconce

NM sheathed
cable

6×6
Pressure-treated
post wrapped in
1× cedar

2×8
Cedar

1×6
Cedar

Stucco finish over
concrete block

▲ Protective structures need not be watertight. This framework of western red cedar timbers and lath screens the sunlight but is consistent with the overall design intent—to retain a close connection with the natural setting. It's really only one step removed from sitting under a canopy of trees, the intended effect.

Getting started

Any one of the features from this project would improve the livability of a backyard. Together they make a great ensemble, but building the package requires good planning.

How you build the tiers of the patio area will dictate a starting point. You can excavate areas for each level if you have a gently sloping site like this one. If not, you may need to bring in fill dirt and tamp it. Find the spot for the fire pit and work outward from there. *(For details on constructing the fire pit, see page 74.)* As you form and pour the slabs on different levels, leave some space for transition steps between them so

movement or settling of one slab doesn't create pressure on the next. Use bender board to create the contours you want.

If you are surfacing the slab with stone or brick, be sure to add the thickness of it and its mortar bed when you plan your excavation depth. Applying stone is similar to laying ceramic tile, although the stone requires a thicker mortar bed (see page 123). Apply the mortar between stones using a grout bag and tool it into the joints as you work. Use a mason's brush to sweep the joints and stones clean as the mortar sets up. As an alternative, set the stone in a bed of wet mortar, then sweep dry mortar mix into the joints and mist generously with a hose, using frequent and repeated applications of water. The water will wick through the dry mortar to create a strong grout joint.

The half-wall for the dining loggia will require some concrete work as well, from the poured footing to the block courses that follow (see page 126). Here the structural requirements are less demanding than for a retaining wall. You may be able to build the block walls directly on the slab. Or you may want to beef up the slab (or footing) by burying rebar in it. You may also want to run vertical lengths of rebar through the blocks. Your local codes may affect this decision, so check them first.

When setting the block, scrape the joints flush rather than concave; the stucco finish will cover them. If you're planning to include electrical outlets or light fixtures such as the ones mounted on the middle posts, run electrical conduit up through the end walls. Fill the hollows in the blocks with concrete and let the assembly cure for several days.

Follow standard process (page 132) to apply stucco to the walls. Keep the block wall damp by using a fine spray from a garden hose, and apply the first (scratch) coat, and rake it with a scarifier. The scratch coat should cure slowly for at least three days; mist the surface regularly to aid the process. If you can't be around to do this, cover the surface with plastic sheeting to slow the moisture loss. Repeated wetting of the

◀ Strong elements in this landscape—from the stone walls to the mix of trees, shrubs, and flowering plants—create a more integrated look for the dining loggia. Take advantage of the power of hard scaping and plants to enhance even the simplest outdoor kitchen designs.

▲ For safety and to keep the fire pit protected from harsh winter weather, a hatch cover made of 2×6 cedar planking covers the pit when it's not in use. The stainless-steel ring caps the ledge of firebricks that line the concrete cylinder.

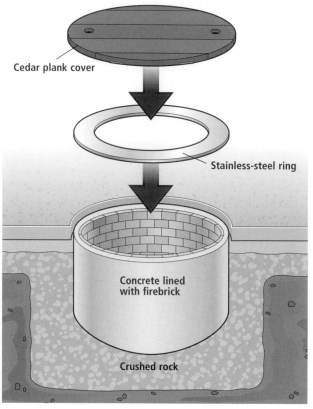

Cedar plank cover

Stainless-steel ring

Concrete lined with firebrick

Crushed rock

▲ The basic anatomy of a fire pit derives from two key objectives: keeping the fire safely contained and preventing water from collecting inside. Set the cylinder in a base of crushed rock so water drains away.

stucco after it has dried only stresses it and makes cracking more likely.

Western cedar was used here for the loggia frame; pressure-treated pine, stained or painted, can be used as an alternative. Use masonry anchors and hot-dipped galvanized screws to fasten the sill to the top of the block wall. On exposed timber structures like this, standard metal framing hardware can look tacky, so use cut joints to connect the frame members. For example, the front and rear beams are notched to hold the joists, which get blind-nailed in place (see page 72).

Fire pit basics

Fire pits are an irresistable element in outdoor landscapes, probably because they evoke images of our frontier past.

In civilized settings, however, they aren't always welcome. Concerns about air quality and fire safety in many urban areas have resulted in bans or restrictions on outdoor fires, especially in open pits. Check local codes and ordinances before you include this feature in your project.

If no legal hurdles present themselves, this version offers a good example to follow. A cast-in-place concrete pit, lined with firebrick, sits at the center of a concrete slab. (A precast concrete cylinder, such as a section of drainpipe, could be used as an alternative.) Drainage is also critical. This installation on the sloped site includes a drain manifold and pipe that empties downhill. If that's not possible on your site, lay a drainage bed of crushed rock under the pit.

Project sequence

To keep the project manageable, break the construction process into stages: the fire pit, the stepped slabs, the planters, and the loggia. Ask your local building officials about required inspections.

■ Determine locations of fire pit, planters, and dining area; measure site.

■ Use rope or garden hose to outline area of contoured slabs. Excavate and grade slab areas.

■ Dig hole for fire pit; add drainpipe (if required) and base of crushed rock.

■ Form and pour concrete surround (or set precast concrete cylinder).

■ Set forms for patio slabs and steps; run underground conduit.

■ Pour concrete slabs and steps. Include reinforced edge if slab will support loggia walls, or use separate footing for walls.

■ If required, pour footing for loggia walls.

■ Apply stone or brick to slab (if desired).

■ Line pit with firebrick; add hatch cover.

■ Construct planter walls with stone.

■ Construct concrete block walls.

■ Apply stucco scratch coat and finish coat.

■ Cap walls with 2×8 cedar sills.

■ Cut joinery in pergola beams and joists.

■ Assemble pergola; top with 2×2 cedar lath.

ESSENTIALS

PRIMARY SKILLS REQUIRED:

FORMING AND POURING A CONCRETE WALL FOOTING AND A CONCRETE SLAB; LAYING BLOCK; MORTARING FLAGSTONE OR BRICK.

TOOLS TO OWN OR RENT:

WATER LEVEL OR TRANSIT; WET-CUTTING MASONRY SAW; CONCRETE FINISHING TOOLS.

MATERIALS:

FORM LUMBER; SAND; GRAVEL; READY MIX CONCRETE; CONCRETE BLOCK; REBAR; MORTAR; STONE; BRICK PAVERS.

◄ A natural outdoor setting such as this wouldn't be well served by an elaborate outdoor kitchen full of bell-and-whistle features. The simple design of this outdoor kitchen allows the space to blend into its natural surroundings.

PROJECT 5
POOLSIDE DINING

This outdoor kitchen gives waterfront dining new meaning, and it does so with a compact footprint—a critical feature if the pool covers much real estate in the backyard. It's hard to imagine a design that offers more convenience. The proximity to the indoor kitchen means virtually any supplies or cooking tools are close at hand, though there's little that can't be found here. These homeowners opted for a prep sink near the grill, rather than a side burner. That choice hinges on your cooking priorities, and with a kitchen range just inside, the trade-off does no harm.

Seating at the raised-counter bar provides a relaxing spot to eat or talk with the cook. The U-shape kitchen layout provides the basic amenities for an outdoor chef: a 30-inch gas grill with an exhaust fan above, two storage cabinets, the prep sink, an icemaker, and an undercounter refrigerator. All these features fit neatly into a small package, and because it's attached to the house, it requires much less construction as a similar freestanding design. The retractable awning provides shade for diners as well as some protection from weather for the kitchen.

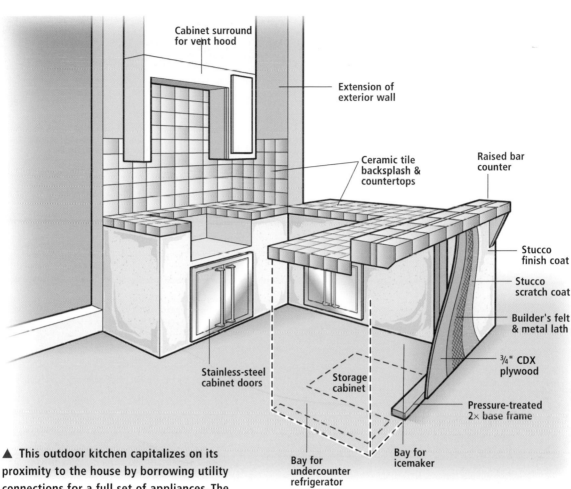

Cabinet surround for vent hood

Extension of exterior wall

Ceramic tile backsplash & countertops

Raised bar counter

Stucco finish coat

Stucco scratch coat

Builder's felt & metal lath

¾" CDX plywood

Pressure-treated 2× base frame

Stainless-steel cabinet doors

Storage cabinet

Bay for undercounter refrigerator

Bay for icemaker

▲ This outdoor kitchen capitalizes on its proximity to the house by borrowing utility connections for a full set of appliances. The base cabinets were built using standard 2× framing lumber sheathed with plywood and finished with stucco.

▶ When planning for an outdoor kitchen that will be attached to or near the house, design it to avoid disruptions in normal traffic patterns. This plan keeps the kitchen's work core and dining counter out of the path through the back door.

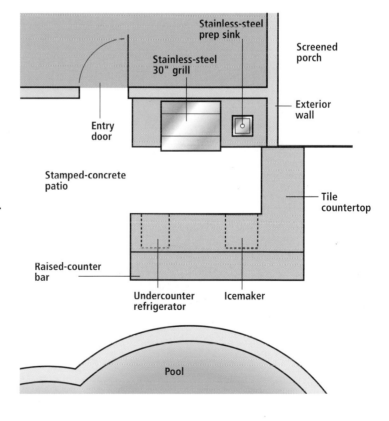

Stainless-steel prep sink

Stainless-steel 30" grill

Screened porch

Entry door

Exterior wall

Stamped-concrete patio

Tile countertop

Raised-counter bar

Undercounter refrigerator

Icemaker

Pool

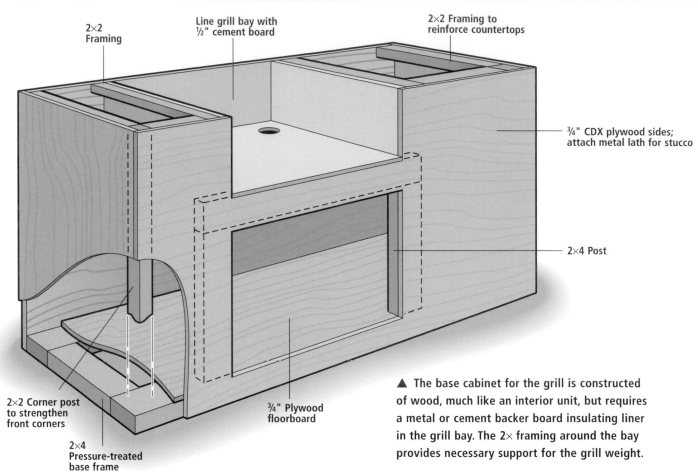

2×2 Framing

Line grill bay with ½" cement board

2×2 Framing to reinforce countertops

¾" CDX plywood sides; attach metal lath for stucco

2×4 Post

2×2 Corner post to strengthen front corners

2×4 Pressure-treated base frame

¾" Plywood floorboard

▲ The base cabinet for the grill is constructed of wood, much like an interior unit, but requires a metal or cement backer board insulating liner in the grill bay. The 2× framing around the bay provides necessary support for the grill weight.

Getting started

Outdoor kitchens attached directly to a house, such as this one, have several advantages. Construction of several features is simpler, because part of the structure for the kitchen already exists. In this case, the glass enclosure around the pool provides additional protection from the weather. Pools mean water and humidity, so decisions about materials and construction need to consider durability as well as function, simplicity, and aesthetics.

On this project the concrete pool deck provides an existing foundation to build upon. Rather than the poured, trenched footing used for other projects featured in this book, but it doesn't have to be. The kitchen walls are smaller and, more important, the protected environment of the pool enclosure allows for

wood-frame rather than masonry construction, so the walls are much lighter as well.

Attaching the kitchen directly to an exterior wall somewhat limits your options for placement. Aim for an area reasonably close to a doorway, but don't have the kitchen straddle the entrance or you'll create traffic headaches. This installation gets it right; there's convenient access to and from the kitchen, but the main traffic is routed off to the side.

Once you've settled on a practical location, use a stud finder to locate studs and other framing members in the existing wall. You will need them for attaching the base and wall cabinets and for anchoring the peninsula that houses the storage and appliances. (On this house a short wall extension creates a niche for the grill area.) In most instances you'll want to

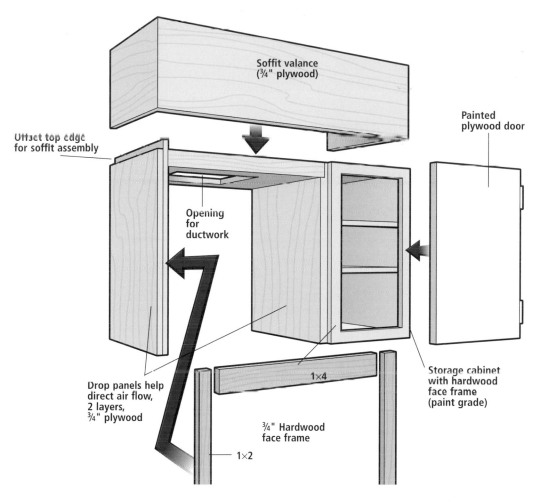

Soffit valance
(¾" plywood)

Offset top edge
for soffit assembly

Opening
for
ductwork

Painted
plywood door

Drop panels help
direct air flow,
2 layers,
¾" plywood

¾" Hardwood
face frame

1×4

1×2

Storage cabinet
with hardwood
face frame
(paint grade)

◀ Build the wall cabinet assembly in separate sections—the storage cabinet with door, the soffit enclosure for the vent ductwork, and the surround for the vent hood, capped with a face frame.

remove the siding material from the section of wall that the kitchen will occupy. Leave any housewrap and sheathing intact.

Building the cabinetry

Conventional interior kitchen cabinets typically feature a hardwood face frame and veneered plywood panels. The base cabinets on this project feature a stucco finish, which calls for different construction methods. The key here is providing a sturdy base for the grill and the countertops. In addition, flexing is bad news for stucco, so the sheathing must be rigid. Use ¾-inch CDX plywood fastened with deck screws to a frame of pressure-treated 2× lumber. Staple a wrap of builder's felt and wire mesh to the surface and apply the stucco in two coats (see page 132).

For the painted wall cabinets (above), stick to more standardized construction. Affix a hardwood face frame (poplar is a good choice for paint-grade trim) to plywood cabinet boxes. The plywood for these cabinets should be a sanded fir (AB grade) or a birch hardwood plywood—something that offers a good surface for painting. The right-hand section of this assembly (with door) is the only true cabinet component; the other section is of the wall cabinet is a surround for the vent hood, which extends up into a bulkhead. Install the entire wall assembly before applying a backsplash material, such as ceramic tile. The base cabinet on the outside leg of the peninsula gets a similar treatment for its interior facade—painted wood rather than stucco. An open storage bay faces the work core of the kitchen and warrants a painted finish.

Countertops and backsplash

The tile countertops present another good do-it-yourself opportunity (see page138). To build the base for tiling, fasten a plywood substrate on top of base cabinets. Attach cement backer board for the countertop (it may also be required inside the grill bay as an insulator). Plan and dry-lay the tiles. Apply thinset mortar with a notched trowel and press the tiles in place. Then grout. Use a similar method for the backsplash area of the wall. Sheathing on the house's exterior wall typically supports the cement backer board.

If you look closely at the tiered countertop on the peninsula (photo, opposite), you'll notice that it has a small backsplash area made of a row of glass blocks. These are a nice alternative to ceramic tile; they're maintenance-free, and in this case they allow for an unusual feature—a fluorescent light fixture has been installed below, providing attractive uplighting.

Project sequence

Many of the early steps involved in building an attached outdoor kitchen are determined by existing site factors, such as siding type, roof overhang, and location of existing windows and doors. Aside from accommodating those features, the building process is fairly straightforward:

- Determine location of the kitchen; locate utility lines.
- Remove siding on exterior wall; locate studs.
- Make any necessary structural changes or additions to walls and roof framing.
- Evaluate existing slab, if any, or form and pour new concrete slab for kitchen foundation.
- Extend utility connections from the house—gas line, water supply and drain, electrical.
- Build and install wall cabinetry and other painted-wood storage units.
- Build base cabinetry as indicated using manufacturer guidelines for grill opening, access door frames, other accessories; install cabinets.
- Add branch lines/conduit/terminals for utilities inside base cabinets as required.
- Apply scratch coat and finish coat of stucco. Paint or finish as desired.

▲ Preventing smoke and cooking fumes from migrating inside the house is critical when an outdoor kitchen is attached directly. Here, an oversize vent hood (3 inches wider on each side than the grill) with a powerful exhaust fan ensures that stray smoke doesn't get indoors.

- Fasten plywood substrate and cement backer board for countertops and backsplash.
- Install glass-block row in tiered bar counter.
- Install ceramic tile on countertops and backsplash areas; grout.
- Install sink and faucet; connect water supply and drain lines.
- Install vent hood with ductwork and required electrical connections.
- Install grill and connect gas line. Make sure grill bay is lined with backer board or metal insulating liner per manufacturer's directions.
- Install metal access doors in base cabinets.
- Install undercounter icemaker and refrigerator.
- Mount retractable awning on wall above grill.

◀ The peninsula adds to the usefulness of this outdoor kitchen by providing bays for the refrigerator and icemaker, a storage cabinet, and a tiered countertop where diners can sit across from the cook and visit. The glass block between the tiers is lighted by a fixture mounted inside the base cabinet.

RETRACTABLE AWNINGS

If the cost or the ever-present shadow of a permanent overhead structure makes it an undesirable feature for your outdoor kitchen, you needn't resign yourself to getting scorched by the sun. Even before outdoor kitchens became as popular as they are, someone figured out that taming the sun's rays could be done more simply and inexpensively. The rest, as they say, is history, or at least the history of the retractable awning. Supported by a lightweight aluminum frame, these awnings mount to an exterior wall and retract into a roll less than a foot in diameter. When extended, the frame unrolls the acrylic fabric cover outward up to a distance of 10 to 12 feet, depending on the manufacturer and model. Standard units, which sell for as little as $700, operate with a hand crank. Most manufacturers offer motorized units, at an upgrade cost of about $500, that operate via a wall switch or a remote control. The fabric covers come in a variety of solid colors and striped patterns.

For more information on awning manufacturers, see the Resource Guide on page 175.

ESSENTIALS

PRIMARY SKILLS REQUIRED:

FORMING AND POURING A CONCRETE SLAB (OPTIONAL, DEPENDING ON THE SITE); BASIC FRAME CARPENTRY; BASIC CABINETMAKING; INSTALLING CERAMIC TILE; BASIC PLUMBING AND ELECTRICAL SKILLS.

TOOLS TO OWN OR RENT:

BUILDER'S LEVEL; PORTABLE CIRCULAR SAW; TABLE SAW; TILE WET SAW; CORDLESS DRILL/DRIVER.

MATERIALS YOU'LL NEED:

FRAMING LUMBER; EXTERIOR-GRADE PLYWOOD; BUILDER'S FELT WITH WIRE MESH; STUCCO MIX; CABINET-GRADE PLYWOOD; 1x HARDWOOD STOCK FOR FACE FRAMES; CEMENT TILE BACKER BOARD; THINSET MORTAR; CERAMIC TILE; GLASS BLOCK; TILE GROUT.

DINING CENTER STAGE

Every outdoor kitchen, to some extent, is an attempt to duplicate the indoor appliances and facilities most people use to prepare food. In simplest form, that means a source of heat and a work surface; from there the variations can quickly lead to a much grander setting.

This project takes aim at the more ambitious end of the outdoor kitchen spectrum. Its appeal lies in its sophistication and in its ability to be translated into smaller sites and budgets. Consider the gazebo, for example. Spanning 24 feet from wall to wall, it houses the cooking station on one wall and a built-in dining area at its center. Scale the structure down to 12 or 16 feet across and you could still include both the cooking station and a dining table.

The beautiful cooking station of stonework and beaded-board can be duplicated on a more modest scale. Construction of the basic framework and finishing techniques would still apply; the compromises would come in a very livable form—a little less storage space, perhaps, or the omission of the dishwasher or prep sink. The charm of the flagstone patio, the rugged stone, and the crisp white woodwork can still be yours. And even with a low-frills approach, the basic package offers the essentials of a great outdoor kitchen—open views, shelter, a grill, and a place to savor the meals you make.

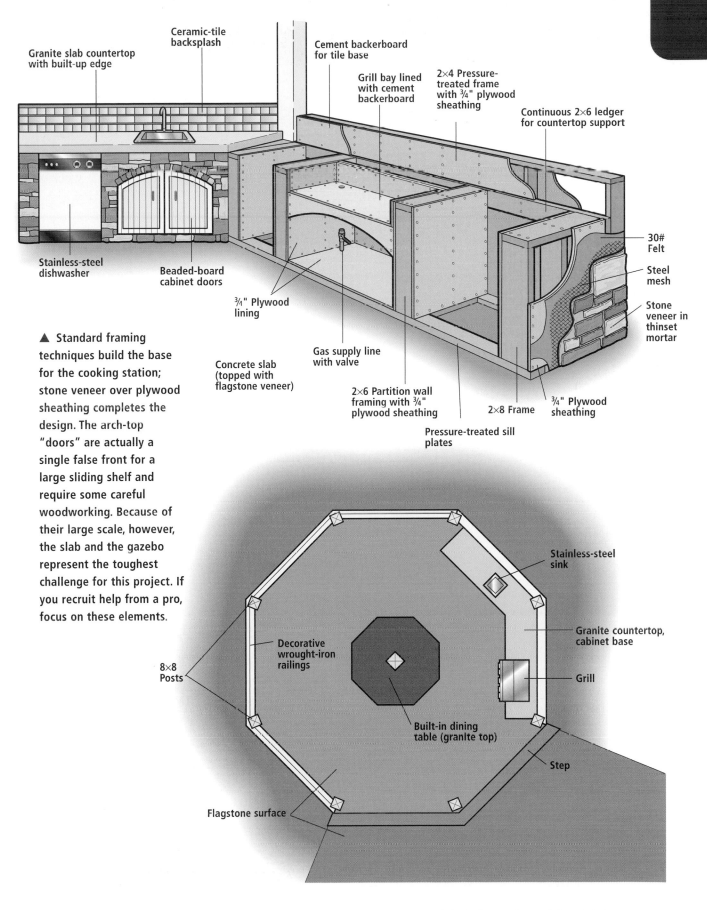

Granite slab countertop
with built-up edge

Ceramic-tile
backsplash

Cement backerboard
for tile base

Grill bay lined
with cement
backerboard

2×4 Pressure-
treated frame
with ¾" plywood
sheathing

Continuous 2×6 ledger
for countertop support

30#
Felt

Steel
mesh

Stone
veneer in
thinset
mortar

Stainless-steel
dishwasher

Beaded-board
cabinet doors

¾" Plywood
lining

▲ Standard framing
techniques build the base
for the cooking station;
stone veneer over plywood
sheathing completes the
design. The arch-top
"doors" are actually a
single false front for a
large sliding shelf and
require some careful
woodworking. Because of
their large scale, however,
the slab and the gazebo
represent the toughest
challenge for this project. If
you recruit help from a pro,
focus on these elements.

Concrete slab
(topped with
flagstone veneer)

Gas supply line
with valve

2×6 Partition wall
framing with ¾"
plywood sheathing

Pressure-treated sill
plates

2×8 Frame

¾" Plywood
sheathing

Stainless-steel
sink

Granite countertop,
cabinet base

Grill

Decorative
wrought-iron
railings

8×8
Posts

Built-in dining
table (granite top)

Step

Flagstone surface

Getting started

This kitchen as shown involves substantial work on the structure before the kitchen itself can be built. The octagonal slab, a step and walkway, and the gazebo frame and roof require skills and experience that are within reach of a do-it-yourselfer, but the scale of the project might make it worthwhile to contract that work to a professional building or landscaping contractor. If you tackle it yourself, be sure to have a roof framing guide, and recruit some help from skilled friends—you'll need extra muscle to handle the large timbers in the frame.

Because the slab (see page 112) directly supports heavy loads around much of its perimeter, the edge of the footing should be substantially thicker than normal, as much as 12 inches thick. You should also include steel reinforcing rod (rebar) around the entire perimeter. You can drill later for masonry anchors to secure the cooking-center base, or plan ahead for the anchor bolt placement along the edges where the bases install. During the pour, set the bolts. (You'll need the completed bases or accurate measurements to determine bolt placement.)

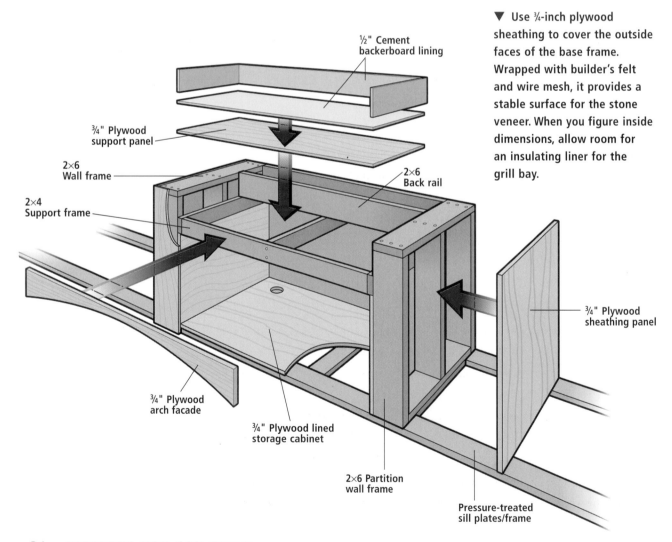

▼ Use ¾-inch plywood sheathing to cover the outside faces of the base frame. Wrapped with builder's felt and wire mesh, it provides a stable surface for the stone veneer. When you figure inside dimensions, allow room for an insulating liner for the grill bay.

½" Cement backerboard lining

¾" Plywood support panel

2×6 Wall frame

2×4 Support frame

2×6 Back rail

¾" Plywood sheathing panel

¾" Plywood arch facade

¾" Plywood lined storage cabinet

2×6 Partition wall frame

Pressure-treated sill plates/frame

▶ Storage space is as much about access and organization as it is about volume. The drawer banks in this cooking center provide plenty of places to sort and divide items and make kitchen supplies more accessible. Full-extension drawer slides (rated to hold up to 100 pounds) are the key.

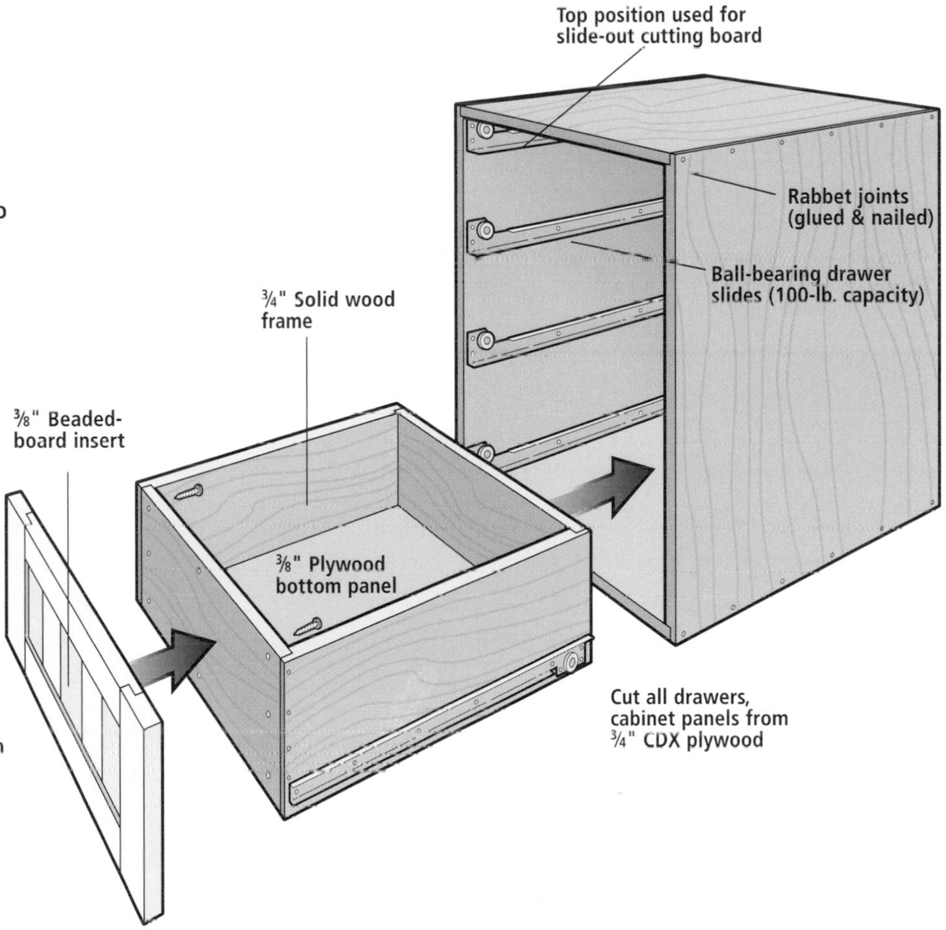

Top position used for slide-out cutting board

Rabbet joints (glued & nailed)

Ball-bearing drawer slides (100-lb. capacity)

¾" Solid wood frame

⅜" Beaded-board insert

⅜" Plywood bottom panel

Fasten drawer face with 1¼" deck screws (through front of drawer box).

Cut all drawers, cabinet panels from ¾" CDX plywood

Set the anchor bolts or brackets for all the posts.

Let the slab cure gradually for several days before setting the posts or other heavy components in place. (For more details on this type of concrete slab work, see Chapter 5: Construction Basics, beginning on page 110.)

Complete both the rough and finish work on the gazebo roof before you install the kitchen, but leave the flagstone patio until later. You want a flat area on the slab where the cooking station goes; after it's installed, you can lay the flagstone around it.

Masonry-only construction is often the preferred method for an outdoor kitchen, but for a project of this scale it would add to an already sizable budget. Because the gazebo roof holds off the worst of the weather, you can use a

wood-frame kitchen base instead. Use pressure-treated lumber and exterior plywood covered with stone veneer. This provides a great look and plenty of protection from the weather.

Use masonry anchors or concrete screws to fasten pressure-treated 2×4 sill plates to the slab. Fashion the cabinet base from a series of box frames covered with plywood sheathing (see illustration opposite). This construction allows flexibility for cabinet sizes and ensures they'll be able to support the heavy granite countertops.

Build modular

There's another advantage to using this type of base construction: The modules that fit inside can be changed or customized to meet different needs. The frame partitions support for the

▲ One of the appealing features of this outdoor kitchen is the massive granite countertop with lots of rooom for food preparation. The grill and appliances have large capacities. A side burner can cook pasta or steam vegetables, and the dishwasher and sink make cleanup quick.

counter, so the spaces between (bays) can accept storage modules that slide in as complete units, such as drawer banks (above).

Tailor the storage modules to how you want access to your outdoor kitchen supplies. At least one bank of drawers is a good idea. Other bays can house a storage cabinet with fixed or sliding shelves, open shelving, and slide-out bins, or they can be fitted with undercounter appliances.

Finishing touches

The granite slab countertops used in this kitchen are probably the most durable material you can choose, but they are not an easy do-it-yourself project. Fabrication requires water-cooled saws with diamond blades and a lot of polishing work. If that's the material you want, have a stone craftsperson come out to measure after the cooking station base is installed, and have this person do the cutting and fitting. This kitchen features a matching center table, another project for the stone fabricator. A ceramic tile backsplash, as shown, certainly qualifies as a do-it-yourself task. Even though the backsplash gets some protection from the gazebo roof, choose vitreous or impervious tile made for outdoor use and install it on cement backer board. It will hold up much better, especially if you get below-freezing temperatures in your area.

The flagstone patio is the final project. Because

of their slightly irregular surfaces, flagstones have to be set in a bed of troweled mortar, not the thinset variety used for tile installation. Brush the mortar joints clean once they've set slightly, and apply a sealer to the patio.

Project sequence

Coordinating the building sequence for this kitchen requires more effort and attention than a smaller-scale project, especially if you have contractors involved for the heavy work. Here's an outline of the basic steps:

- Measure site; mark perimeter of slab.
- Excavate areas for slabs; run underground lines and conduit for utility connections.
- Set forms for slab; add crushed-rock base and compact with a plate compactor.
- Install reinforcing rebar and/or wire mesh.
- Pour and finish slab; set J-bolts for posts at corners and center. Let slab cure 3–7 days.
- Build gazebo frame and roof structure.
- Cover roof frame with sheathing, roofing felt, flashing, and shingles.
- Caulk and paint gazebo as desired.
- Fasten pressure-treated sill plates to slab.
- Use 2× framing lumber and plywood sheathing to build framework for base cabinet.
- Secure cabinet(s) to sill plates.
- Staple builder's felt and wire mesh to exterior surfaces of base cabinets.
- Apply mortar and stone veneer.
- Build modular storage units for cabinets.
- Line grill bay with cement backer board or metal insulating liner.
- Install stone countertops and backsplash tile.
- Set flagstone floor in troweled mortar.
- Paint and install modular storage units.
- Install and connect grill, sink, and appliances.

ESSENTIALS

PRIMARY SKILLS REQUIRED:

FORMING AND POURING A CONCRETE SLAB; ADVANCED FRAME CARPENTRY; BASIC CABINETMAKING; INSTALLING STONE VENEER; BASIC PLUMBING AND ELECTRICAL SKILLS.

TOOLS TO OWN OR RENT:

BUILDER'S TRANSIT OR WATER LEVEL; VIBRATING PLATE COMPACTOR; CONCRETE FINISHING TOOLS; PORTABLE CIRCULAR SAW; TABLE SAW; CORDLESS DRILL/DRIVER.

MATERIALS YOU'LL NEED:

FORM LUMBER; STEEL-WIRE REINFORCEMENT MESH; READY-MIX CONCRETE; FRAMING LUMBER; EXTERIOR-GRADE PLYWOOD SHEATHING; BUILDER'S FELT WITH WIRE MESH; 1× HARDWOOD STOCK FOR FACE FRAMES; CEMENT BACKER BOARD; THINSET MORTAR; STONE VENEER; FLAGSTONE; GRANITE COUNTERTOPS (CUSTOM-FABRICATED); CERAMIC TILE.

▼ The "doors" below the sink disguise an unexpected twist—they are a solid-front panel affixed to a deep sliding shelf. This feature allows storage of larger items and makes the contents more accessible than a cupboard with twin doors and a fixed shelf.

Project 7
All the Angles

Any architect will tell you that one of the key elements in good design is context. The best structures fit their sites so naturally that they seem inevitable, almost as if they grew there like a tree. The same principle applies to any residential project, and this outdoor kitchen gets high marks for its use of setting.

The strong geometry of this kitchen, tucked gracefully between two trees and in front of a lush terrace, blends surprisingly well with the contoured landscape. Some of the credit for this harmony goes to the low-profile silhouette–this kitchen doesn't take up enough vertical space to be intrusive. In addition, the angled layout creates an inconspicuous home for the undercounter appliances. To top it off, the slightly mottled tile with its muted-gray glaze seems lifted directly from the stones and plants on the terrace.

Durable materials are a must for an installation such as this. Exposure to water, wind, and sun point to masonry construction as the ideal choice. Concrete block walls covered with ceramic tile make for a simple "one-piece-at-a-time" building process, but the project calls for some specialized cutting. Plan to rent diamond-blade saws for this project.

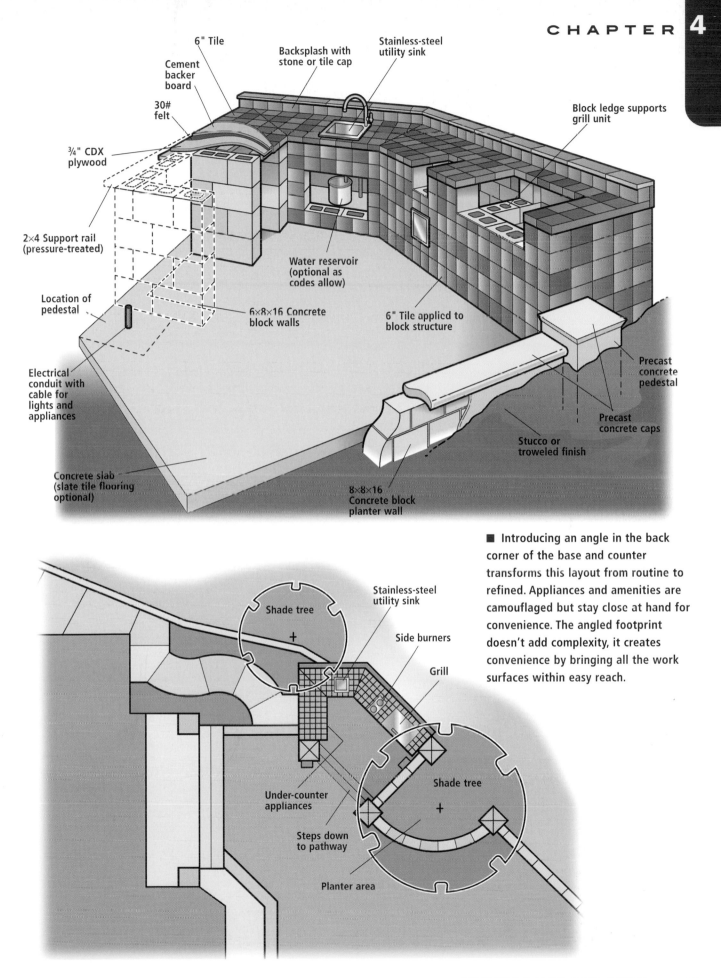

6" Tile

Cement backer board

30# felt

¾" CDX plywood

Backsplash with stone or tile cap

Stainless-steel utility sink

Block ledge supports grill unit

2×4 Support rail (pressure-treated)

Location of pedestal

Water reservoir (optional as codes allow)

6×8×16 Concrete block walls

6" Tile applied to block structure

Electrical conduit with cable for lights and appliances

Precast concrete pedestal

Precast concrete caps

Stucco or troweled finish

Concrete slab (slate tile flooring optional)

8×8×16 Concrete block planter wall

Shade tree

Stainless-steel utility sink

Side burners

Grill

Under-counter appliances

Steps down to pathway

Planter area

Shade tree

■ Introducing an angle in the back corner of the base and counter transforms this layout from routine to refined. Appliances and amenities are camouflaged but stay close at hand for convenience. The angled footprint doesn't add complexity, it creates convenience by bringing all the work surfaces within easy reach.

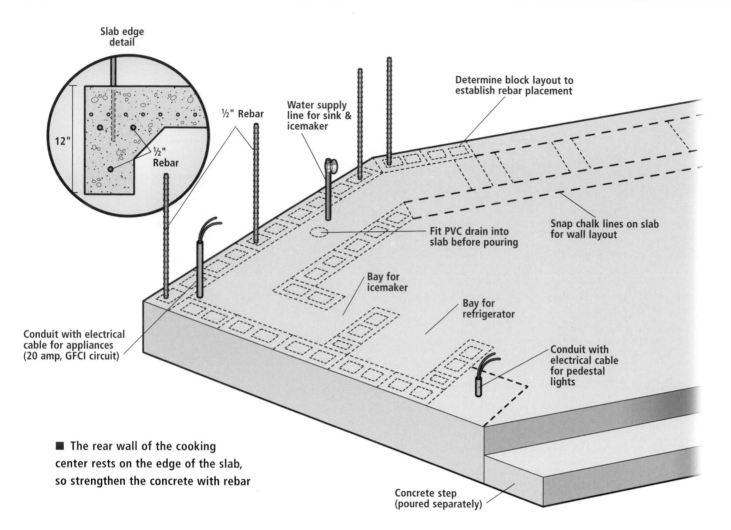

Slab edge detail

12"

½" Rebar

½" Rebar

Water supply line for sink & icemaker

Determine block layout to establish rebar placement

Fit PVC drain into slab before pouring

Snap chalk lines on slab for wall layout

Bay for icemaker

Bay for refrigerator

Conduit with electrical cable for appliances (20 amp, GFCI circuit)

Conduit with electrical cable for pedestal lights

■ The rear wall of the cooking center rests on the edge of the slab, so strengthen the concrete with rebar

Concrete step (poured separately)

Getting started

A poured 4-inch-thick slab (see page 112) is adequate for the floor area in front of the cooking center, but you'll need to pour a 12-inch footing on the rear wall. Pay special attention to soil stability and the likelihood of frost heave; an all-masonry structure such as this can't flex the way a wood-frame structure can. Dig out as much soil as necessary to set a drainage bed of compacted crushed rock throughout the entire excavation. When setting forms, create a slight slope (2 percent) to promote drainage off the slab; if possible, also grade away from the kitchen to keep excess moisture from collecting in the soil, reducing the likelihood of cracks.

Using steel-wire mesh to reinforce the slab will help prevent cracking. Use rebar around the edges where the heaviest loads will be concentrated. Before pouring concrete, place any utility lines or conduit for electrical cable. The project plan shows a sink drain line embedded in the slab, which requires a connection to the home's sewer system. For sites where tying in the kitchen drain is impractical or prohibitively expensive, a gravel-filled dry well may serve the purpose. Be sure to check local codes.

After setting the forms but before the concrete pour, measure for the block layout (or mock up a dry run with a course of block) and determine where the hollow bays will fall (above). Mark these points on the forms and use them as guides to place vertical rebar in the slab.

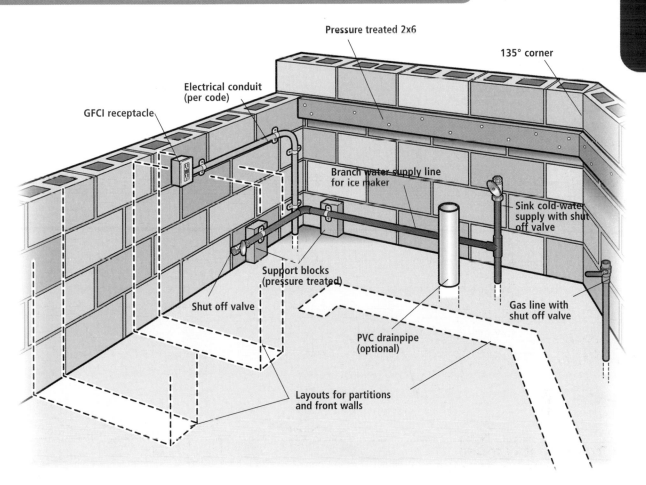

Pressure treated 2x6

135° corner

Electrical conduit
(per code)

GFCI receptacle

Branch water supply line
for ice maker

Sink cold-water
supply with shut
off valve

Support blocks
(pressure treated)

Shut off valve

Gas line with
shut off valve

PVC drainpipe
(optional)

Layouts for partitions
and front walls

▲ If the kitchen includes a full complement of utility connections, placement of a gas line, water supply line, and conduit for electrical cable must be done during the rough stages of construction. This illustration shows the option of a drainpipe, which requires connection to a main drain/sewer line. If this proves too difficult or costly, a portable reservoir can substitute.

Use wire to tie them to the footing before the pour, or place them when the concrete starts to firm up a little. Add a light broom texture to the slab, then let it cure for a week before setting any block. Leave the forms on for several days.

Set the block

When the slab has cured, snap chalk lines to mark the layout of all the wall edges and corners (see page 126). The angled design will require cutting some blocks at a 45-degree angle; it's worth renting a wet-cutting masonry block saw for this part of the project.

Trowel a mortar bed slightly wider than the block onto the slab and set the first course of

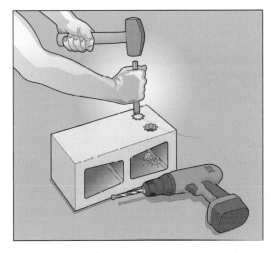

◄ To clear a path for utility lines, use a masonry bit to drill ¼-inch holes into a ring pattern about 1½ inches in diameter. Punch the hole out with a hammer and masonry chisel.

block for the back walls. Build lead corners for these walls, then run mason's lines and fill in the field blocks between them. Tool the mortar

▶ A separate side burner is a welcome feature for remote outdoor kitchens, where distance from the house makes the convenience of a well-equipped cooking center even more valuable. A stainless-steel cover protects this unit from weather when it's not in use.

joints flush as you work; the interior faces of the walls won't show, and the outer faces will be covered with ceramic tile.

Next build the partition walls, the short support walls in the grill bay, and the pocket for a side burner. As you build these interior walls, note the placement of the water supply line, gas line, and electrical conduit. If your installation has any blocks that will intersect those lines, mark the pipe location on each side of the block and drill a series of ¼-inch holes into a ring pattern about 1½ inches in diameter (see page 91). Punch the hole out with a hammer and chisel to clear a path for the utility lines, then set the block. When all the walls are finished and the pipes and conduit are placed, pour concrete into the cells of the block to create solid walls.

The tile surfaces

The countertop uses a 2×4 framework capped with ¾-inch plywood as a substrate for cement backerboard and the ceramic tile (see page 138). Bolt a pressure-treated 2×6 ledger in place on the rear walls to support the back of the countertop. (The rear walls extend above this height to create a backsplash behind the counter.)

Cover the plywood with a layer of builder's felt, followed by ½-inch cement backer board and the tile, bedded in thinset mortar. This "sandwich" of materials totals about 3 inches thick. Buy edge tiles wide enough for the job, or cut field tiles if edging isn't available.

Use vitreous or impervious tile and apply two coats of sealer to the grout lines so they stay clean and dry.

◀ Steaming, boiling, and other stove-top cooking methods can be done on the side burner, but the characteristic flavor that comes from grilling means most foods will end up on the grill.

When the countertop is complete, add tile to the block walls. In this project thinset mortar can be applied directly to the block.

Patio and planter

Rather than mimic this patio and planter design exactly, try to achieve the basics of what these features do—complement the other colors and textures of the kitchen and landscaping. The broom-textured concrete slab doesn't need covering, but random-size pieces of tumbled marble and stone provide a rich look for the patio. The rounded caps and the small pedestal columns on the planter feature a friendly, timeworn look, thanks to the use of stone components. Just as the cooking center, the planter walls and pedestals can be built with concrete block and covered with veneer of another material. It keeps the costs down and the construction simple.

Project sequence

Although this project has several unique features, almost all of its construction revolves around the repetition of a few techniques and materials. Here's how the sequence unfolds:

■ Measure site and mark perimeter lines.

■ Run underground utilities to site.

■ Excavate and grade for slab; add and compact crushed rock for drainage bed.

■ Set forms and fit steel reinforcements.

■ Pour and finish slab; let cure one week.

■ Measure and mark layout for kitchen walls.

■ Lay first course of block for outer walls; build lead corners, then complete to full height.

■ Build interior partition and support walls.

■ Run conduit/pipe; add outlets and valves.

■ Bolt 2×6 ledger to rear wall for countertop.

■ Complete block walls for front of kitchen, with

◄ A compact outdoor refrigerator and icemaker nest conveniently under the countertop, so everything is close at hand for a cook or diner. The door at the right provides access to the sink connections and a storage area.

bays for grill and side burner, access openings.

■ Build 2× frame for countertop; sheathe with ¾-inch plywood; add builder's felt.

■ Fasten cement backer board on plywood.

■ Set ceramic tile in thinset mortar on counter.

■ Cover block walls with ceramic tile.

■ Grout and seal all grout lines.

■ Hook up supply and drain lines to prep sink.

■ Install access doors on front walls.

■ Install grill, side burner, sink, and appliances.

ESSENTIALS

PRIMARY SKILLS REQUIRED:

FORMING AND POURING A CONCRETE SLAB; LAYING CONCRETE BLOCK; BASIC CARPENTRY SKILLS; INSTALLING CERAMIC TILE; BASIC PLUMBING AND ELECTRICAL SKILLS.

TOOLS TO OWN OR RENT:

BUILDER'S LEVEL; CONCRETE-FINISHING TOOLS; WET-CUTTING MASONRY/BLOCK SAW; PORTABLE CIRCULAR SAW; CORDLESS DRILL/DRIVER; TILE CUTTER OR TILE SAW.

MATERIALS YOU'LL NEED:

FORM LUMBER; READY-MIX CONCRETE; EXTERIOR-GRADE ¾-INCH PLYWOOD; BUILDER'S FELT; CEMENT TILE BACKER BOARD; THINSET MORTAR; CERAMIC TILE; TILE GROUT; GAS PIPE AND WATER SUPPLY/DRAINPIPE; ELECTRICAL CONDUIT.

OUT IN THE WOODS

B rick, tile, stone, and concrete often take center stage in outdoor kitchen design. Certainly their durability and good looks justify their popularity, but this project offers evidence that masonry isn't your only option.

Designed and built by a woodworker, the outdoor kitchen in this backyard rests inconspicuously on a two-level deck made with the builder's favorite material: a dense tropical hardwood called ipe, harvested from a certified managed forest in Brazil.

Ipe boasts a list of traits that recommend it for outdoor projects. First, it's naturally resistant to decay from moisture, fungus, insects, and almost every other natural enemy of wood, including fire. (It will burn under the right

circumstances, but it's as close to fireproof as wood gets.) It's extremely durable and wear-resistant—though tough to machine—and pound-for-pound stronger than steel. It has a rich reddish-brown color, similar to mahogany, that can be maintained with applications of sealer.

This design offers plenty of other options as well, from traditional woods such as cedar to an entire generation of new composite materials, all engineered to be more durable and stable than natural wood. Whatever materials you prefer, the approach taken here shows that simple but well-chosen amenities can make any deck into a versatile platform for outdoor cooking and dining. Bricks and stones aren't the only bones for building outside. This project shows that wood decks are contenders too.

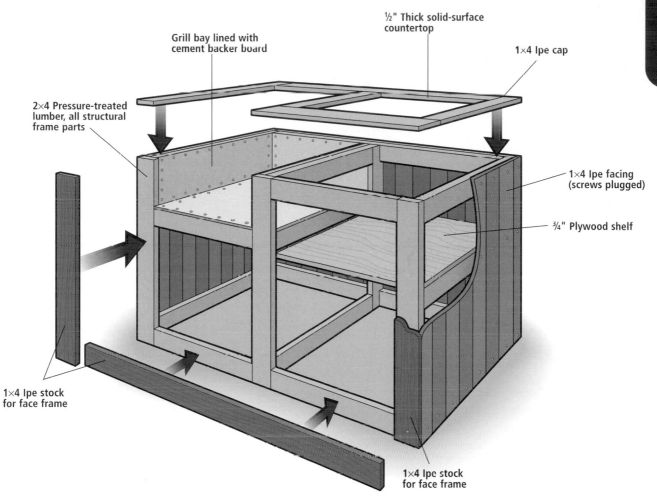

½" Thick solid-surface countertop

Grill bay lined with cement backer board

1×4 Ipe cap

2×4 Pressure-treated lumber, all structural frame parts

1×4 Ipe facing (screws plugged)

¾" Plywood shelf

1×4 Ipe stock for face frame

1×4 Ipe stock for face frame

Getting started

A raised deck such as this one offers more flexibility than ground-level masonry installations. First the terrain isn't as critical. Concrete pier footings can be placed where needed and where site conditions allow, even if the area is sloped or otherwise irregular. With a detached design such as this, the deck's orientation and proportions can be easily altered, and other sections or levels can be added using the same basic building methods (see page 144).

After selecting your site, measure the area for the deck and drive stakes to mark the corner and pier locations. Use batter boards and mason's line to lay out the precise outline and the locations of the concrete piers. Your working drawings for the deck should include a layout of the piers, posts, beams, and joists.

▼ Basic construction techniques work best with a hardwood such as ipe. The frame for this cooking center is pressure-treated pine, hidden in a wrap of ipe planking. The doors feature tongue-and-groove joints.

Dig 12-inch-diameter footing holes to below the frostline (check local codes) and add 6 inches of crushed rock in each for drainage. Rent a power auger and recruit some help to dig the footing holes; the cost is a small price to pay for saving time and reducing the most back-breaking work of the project.

When the holes are ready, drop in cardboard tube forms (10- or 12-inch diameter). Use stakes and braces to hold the forms in place with the tops about 2 inches above grade. Try to make the tops of the forms as level to each other as possible; this will help in cutting the posts and will give the project a neater appearance.

Calculate the concrete volume you'll need for all the piers; the forms usually indicate how many cubic feet of concrete are required for each foot of depth. Most ready-mix companies deliver only large loads, so for a smaller project you may mix your own in a tub, wheelbarrow, or rented mixer. Install anchor bolts in the center of each pier after the concrete sets up slightly, then let them cure for a week before you start building the frame.

The deck frame

After the concrete pier footings have had a chance to cure, reset the mason's lines on the batter boards and align and bolt the metal post anchors in place on each pier. On this project the homeowner used 2×6 pressure-treated pine to make sandwich-construction posts for the interior piers, but the perimeter posts are ipe (also made from 2× stock bolted together).

LOWER DECK
(9" lower than upper deck)

Fire pit

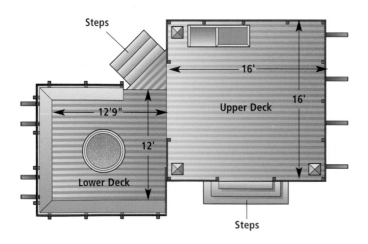

◄ **Offset frames and staggered platform heights add visual interest to the deck but don't require complicated shapes or sophisticated engineering. This layout also creates natural zones for different activities on the deck. The smaller lower deck is a perfect place for light snacks, appetizers before dinner, or dessert and conversation after. Cooking and dining occupy the upper deck.**

Steps

16'

16'

Upper Deck

12'9"

12'

Lower Deck

Steps

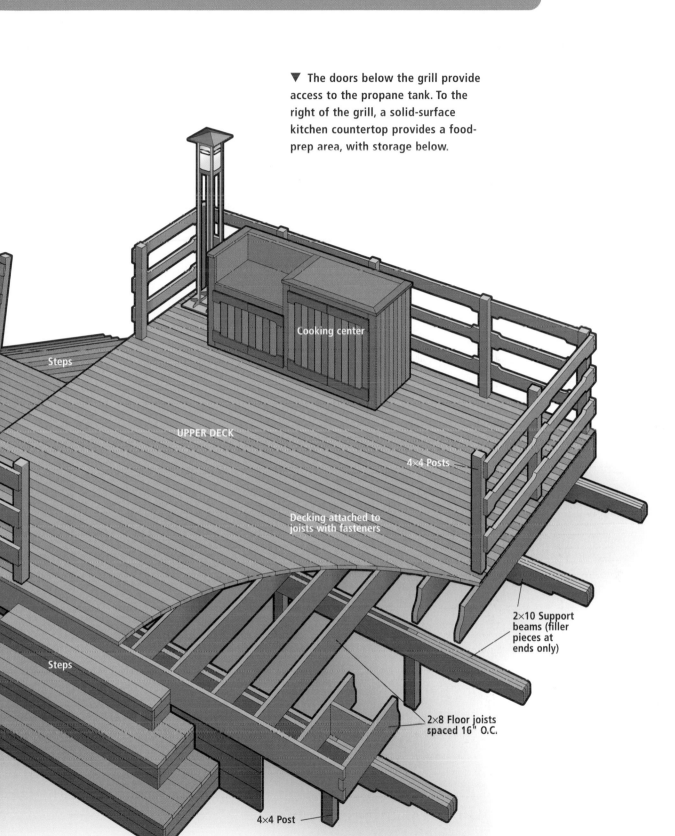

▼ The doors below the grill provide access to the propane tank. To the right of the grill, a solid-surface kitchen countertop provides a food-prep area, with storage below.

Cooking center

Steps

UPPER DECK

4×4 Posts

Decking attached to joists with fasteners

Steps

2×10 Support beams (filler pieces at ends only)

2×8 Floor joists spaced 16" O.C.

4×4 Post

All of the fascia and skirt boards are ipe, so when the decking and railings are installed the pressure-treated framework is hidden.

Add the decking

As composite and premium hardwood decking have gained popularity, many deck builders and designers have abandoned the use of nails and screws in favor of "blind" fastening systems. These systems require specialty hardware that secure the decking from below or along its side edges, so no fasteners are visible from above. (For more on these alternate fastening systems, see page 147.)

For this project the homeowner used small plastic (see illustration below). To install them you need a biscuit joiner (a portable power tool that cuts a small slot in the edge of the board) and a cordless drill. As each deck board is installed, a cleat is fastened to each joist, and the side fins are inserted into the slots in the edge of the decking.

Keep in mind that some sections of the deck will have railing posts bolted to the inside of the rim joists. These should be installed before the decking material goes on.

Bench and railings

Aside from altering the shape of the deck or building multiple levels, the railing offers the best opportunity for personalizing a design. For platforms that sit above a certain height (usually 30 inches from grade), building codes require railings and specify that the space between railing parts not allow a small child to become entrapped or fall through.

This railing design is based on early 20th-century designs of architects Charles and Henry Greene, with their signature "cloudlift" contour along the horizontal edges.

Similar detailing is used along the bench backrests, which feature canted posts bolted to the outside of the rim joists. The bench seats and backrest rails are made with the same 1×4 planking used for the decking. Because ipe is difficult to machine, keep the detailing simple if you opt for this material. A round-over router bit leaves a comfortable contour on the edges.

▼ The fire pit is the favorite element of this outdoor environment, adding cooking function as well as atmosphere. A precast concrete cylinder forms the surround, which is lined with firebrick and filled halfway with rock for drainage.

DECK BOARD FASTENERS

▶ Plastic fastening clips were used to secure the decking boards. Screwed to the joists, the clips have side fins that fit into slots routed in the edge of the decking boards.

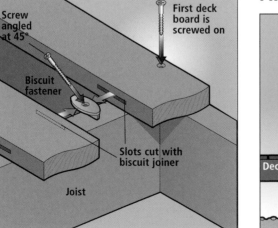

Screw angled at 45°

First deck board is screwed on

Biscuit fastener

Slots cut with biscuit joiner

Joist

FIRE PIT

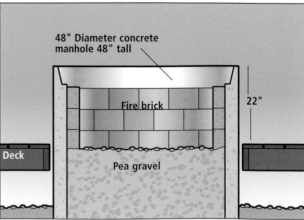

48" Diameter concrete manhole 48" tall

Fire brick

22"

Deck

Pea gravel

Project sequence

This project involves everything from rough grading and excavating to precision woodworking. Here's how to proceed:

- Measure site and set stakes for deck footprint.
- Set batter boards at each corner and run lines to lay out the locations of concrete piers.
- Excavate footing holes to required depth; set cardboard tube forms level with each other; secure with stakes and temporary braces.
- Pour concrete; install anchor bolts when firm. Let concrete cure for 7 days.
- Trench for underground electrical conduit and place conduit with a pull line inside.
- Align and bolt metal post bases in place.
- Notch top ends of posts to create the shoulder profile for the beam connection.
- Bolt pressure treated posts in place on inside piers; install ipe posts on perimeter footings.
- Excavate area for fire pit and partially fill with gravel or crushed rock.
- Install concrete cylinder for firepit. Fill to halfway mark with gravel; line with firebrick.
- Assemble sandwich beams from 2× stock and bolt in place on posts.
- Build joist framework to support decking; use metal framing hardware and joist hangers for connections.
- Bolt railing posts to inside faces of rim joists where required.
- Install decking; predrill decking if required, or modify as needed for alternate fastening system.
- Cut and install railing components.
- Bolt canted posts for bench backrests to outer face of rim joists; add rest of bench framework and slats for seats and backrests.
- Build steps as required at deck entry.
- Build pressure-treated framework for cooking center; line grill bay with cement backer board.
- Fasten ipe slats on sides and back of cooking center; also use 1×4 ipe for face frame.
- Build and hang frame-and-batten doors.
- Purchase custom countertop from local solid-surfacing fabrication shop; frame with 1× ipe.
- Make electrical connections from underground conduit to light fixtures and/or cooking center.
- Apply clear penetrating oil sealer with ultraviolet-blocker to all exposed ipe surfaces.

◀ The tiered design of the cooking center puts the grill at the proper height and also provides a countertop for preparing food. The solid-surface material is designed for interior use, so a cover was added.

ESSENTIALS

PRIMARY SKILLS REQUIRED:

LAYOUT AND MARKING FOR DECK STRUCTURE; FORMING AND POURING CONCRETE FOOTING PIERS; BASIC CARPENTRY SKILLS; ADVANCED WOODWORKING SKILLS FOR DETAILING OF IPE COMPONENTS; BASIC ELECTRICAL SKILLS.

TOOLS TO OWN OR RENT:

BUILDER'S TRANSIT OR WATER LEVEL; POSTHOLE DIGGER; BUILDER'S LEVEL; PORTABLE CIRCULAR SAW; ROUTER WITH CARBIDE-TIPPED CUTTERS; CORDLESS DRILL; POWER MITER SAW; BISCUIT JOINER (FOR EB-TY FASTENING SYSTEM).

MATERIALS YOU'LL NEED:

CARDBOARD PIER FORMS; READY-MIX CONCRETE; POST BASE HARDWARE AND FRAMING HARDWARE; PRESSURE-TREATED STOCK FOR FRAME; CEMENT BACKER BOARD IPE POSTS, DECKING, AND 2× FRAMING STOCK; SEALER.

GIMME SHELTER

How much use an outdoor kitchen gets depends on many things, from a homeowner's social calendar to the realities of the local climate. If you want to pay less attention to the daily forecast, your kitchen should include features that can ward off unwanted weather. Good design can help you hold your own against sizzling sun, unexpected rain, or chilly breezes, as this project illustrates.

For convenience the kitchen is set on a rear corner of the house, under a roof extension, gaining substantial shelter to begin with. The outer wall includes two sliding windows, which can open to let a cooling breeze flow through or close to shut out unwanted weather. An awning over the dining area offers shade and shelter. A few easy modifications to the design, such as the addition of retractable shutters over the bar, would provide additional weatherproofing for use in harsher climates.

Adding amenities to a kitchen close to the house almost always means lower costs than similar features in a detached or remote kitchen. Water, gas, and electrical lines can be extended through the home's exterior wall.

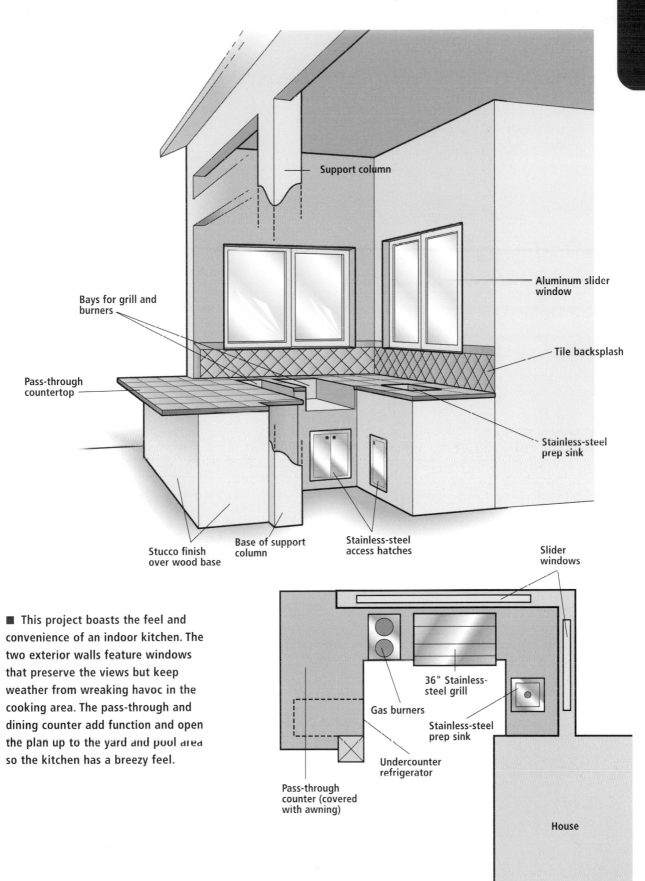

Support column

Aluminum slider window

Tile backsplash

Bays for grill and burners

Pass-through countertop

Stainless-steel prep sink

Stucco finish over wood base

Base of support column

Stainless-steel access hatches

Slider windows

■ This project boasts the feel and convenience of an indoor kitchen. The two exterior walls feature windows that preserve the views but keep weather from wreaking havoc in the cooking area. The pass-through and dining counter add function and open the plan up to the yard and pool area so the kitchen has a breezy feel.

36" Stainless-steel grill

Gas burners

Stainless-steel prep sink

Undercounter refrigerator

Pass-through counter (covered with awning)

House

■ A lot of advance planning ensured this compact layout would have room for all the features the homeowners wanted. The cabinet bases are built to house an undercounter refrigerator, two drawer banks, access doors, the grill, and a side burner.

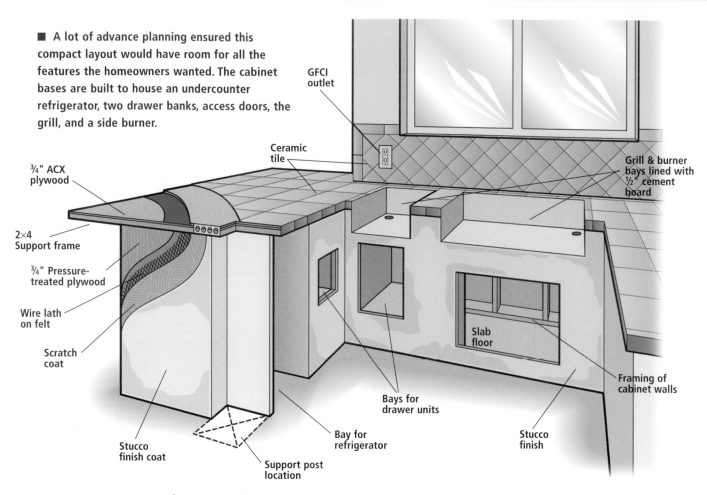

GFCI outlet

Ceramic tile

¾" ACX plywood

2×4 Support frame

¾" Pressure-treated plywood

Wire lath on felt

Scratch coat

Stucco finish coat

Support post location

Bay for refrigerator

Bays for drawer units

Grill & burner bays lined with ½" cement board

Slab floor

Framing of cabinet walls

Stucco finish

Getting started

Thorough planning pays off in many ways. The design improves with revision, the building process goes more smoothly, and the final results are bound to be better. The benefits of careful planning are obvious: an outdoor kitchen so closely tethered to the house that it's nearly a seamless extension.

Attaching an outdoor kitchen to a house means you have to work with what you've got. The existing site conditions, from the siding material and foundation of the home to the locations of electrical and plumbing lines, will play a big role in determining the look and features of the new structure.

This particular kitchen design requires a starting point that almost any home offers: a square outside corner surrounded by a modest patch of level yard space. Given that, you can adapt the basic design to fit your site. Most single-story homes won't have roof edges tall enough to allow for the high ceiling shown here, but the layout itself can probably stay the same.

Pick the corner where you want the kitchen located. You'll want access to utility connections, so stay near the indoor kitchen if possible. If your home has a concrete slab foundation with buried pipes and conduit, making long connections will be more difficult than if you have a basement or a crawlspace, so proximity will be even more important.

Determine the location of studs and other structural framing members in the existing walls, then decide specifically where you want to remove the exterior siding and connect the new kitchen wall. On a stucco exterior, such as the one shown here, a portable circular saw with a masonry blade will cut to the sheathing

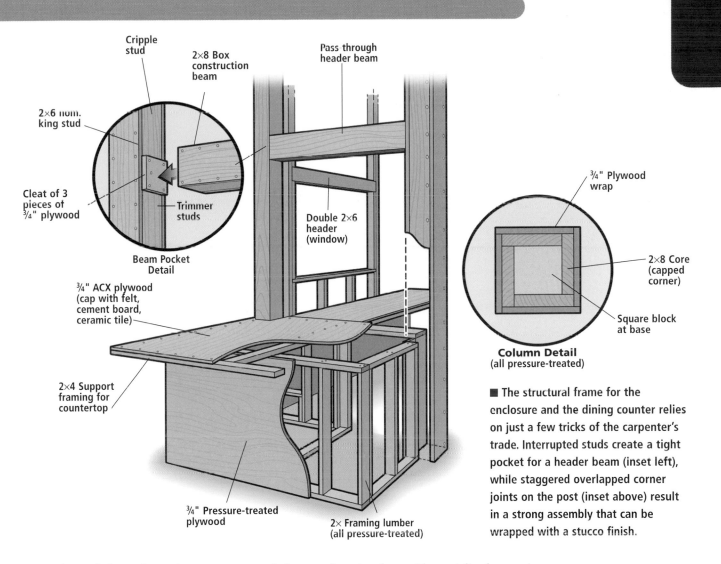

Cripple stud

2×8 Box construction beam

Pass through header beam

2×6 nom. king stud

Cleat of 3 pieces of ¾" plywood

Trimmer studs

Beam Pocket Detail

Double 2×6 header (window)

¾" ACX plywood (cap with felt, cement board, ceramic tile)

2×4 Support framing for countertop

¾" Pressure-treated plywood

2× Framing lumber (all pressure-treated)

¾" Plywood wrap

2×8 Core (capped corner)

Square block at base

Column Detail (all pressure-treated)

■ The structural frame for the enclosure and the dining counter relies on just a few tricks of the carpenter's trade. Interrupted studs create a tight pocket for a header beam (inset left), while staggered overlapped corner joints on the post (inset above) result in a strong assembly that can be wrapped with a stucco finish.

beneath the surface, where you can attach the new framing. Whatever the existing siding and trim, match the details on your outdoor kitchen.

The footprint

Once you know where you're going to build, set stakes to establish the footprint of the kitchen. It should allow for the roof above, whether it's an extension of the house roof or a structure added to the exterior wall. An attached outdoor kitchen can sit on a slab, an insulated slab with a deep perimeter footing, or a stemwall with a footing. In colder regions the foundation under the outdoor kitchen should match that of the house, at least in its resistance to frost heaving.

Start framing the kitchen by setting pressure-treated sill plates on the slab and

fastening them with specialized concrete screws or masonry anchors.

Framing walls

The window openings of this cooking center make for a little cutting and fitting, but the geometry is simple. Even though much of the structure is actually a base cabinet for the cooking gear, build it all as if you were framing standard walls (see page 150). Bottom and top plates, studs, trimmers, and headers will provide the cabinet shape you need while creating a sturdy assembly that can handle any weight from the roof structure. Use pressure-treated lumber. Sheath the frame with ⅝ inch or thicker CDX plywood and a layer of builder's felt or housewrap. This project was finished with

▲ Are you indoors or out? It's actually a little of both, and that dual personality makes this project successful. One or two cooks can occupy the sheltered cooking center and still enjoy views and cool breezes through the windows. A pass-through opening and a large dining counter provide access for serving and eating. Low-maintenance surfaces make cleaning easy.

stucco to match the house; in that case, you'd need to add wire mesh or metal lath also.

An overall view of the framing is provided in the illustration on page 103, but you can vary this depending on your site factors and the code requirements in your area. The large post and the box beam over the bar counter are both built from thinner stock, but are adequate for their duties. As for the windows, install units with aluminum or vinyl frames; they won't require painting and can be cleaned on the outside simply by hosing them off. The best type for this use is a horizontal sliding unit; the sash operating hardware is simpler than a double-hung window and not affected by water.

Tile and trim

The counter frames involve a construction method similar to the walls; use 2×4 stock for the base and ¾-inch plywood for the panels. You need a subassembly that won't flex with normal use or from the weight of the tile. Secure these frames to the base cabinet, then add cement backer board. (Backer board is also used to line the grill bay and side burner bay; you can substitute metal insulating liners if the manufacturer's instructions allow.) Use vitreous or impervious tile for the countertops and backsplash, and apply a sealer after grouting.

▶ A side burner paired with a bank of stainless-steel drawers for cooking utensils makes it possible to prepare a complete meal outdoors. Features such as these add to the project cost but create a self-contained cooking center.

Project sequence

Because many of the structural connections and design details for this project are site-specific, it's likely you'll have to modify them for your own home. Here's the general outline of steps:

- Set perimeter stakes to define project area.
- Locate framing members in existing walls.
- Strip siding where kitchen wall will connect.
- Excavate and grade for slab or foundation.
- Set forms; add rebar and wire mesh as needed.
- Pour concrete and finish slab; let cure a week.
- Fasten pressure-treated sill plates for layout.
- Build full-height "enclosure" walls for kitchen, including window framing and end post. Secure as required to existing exterior wall.
- Build roof frame, sheathe, and shingle.
- Extend branch lines for gas, water, electrical.
- Frame and sheathe the base cabinet sections.
- Build and install countertop substrate panels.
- Apply felt with wire mesh for stucco surfaces.
- Install windows and window trim.
- Apply scratch and finish coats of stucco.
- Install cement backer board on countertops, backsplash area, and, if required, as insulating liners in grill bay and side burner bay.
- Set ceramic tile (in thinset mortar) on the countertops and backsplash. Grout and seal.
- Install prep sink and connect supply/drain.
- Install grill and side burner; connect gas lines.
- Install access doors and drawer banks.
- Install undercounter refrigerator.
- Order fabric awning with frame to fit over dining counter area. Install when completed.

ESSENTIALS

PRIMARY SKILLS REQUIRED:

FORMING AND POURING A CONCRETE SLAB; WALL AND ROOF FRAMING; BASIC CARPENTRY SKILLS; INSTALLING CERAMIC TILE; BASIC PLUMBING AND ELECTRICAL SKILLS.

TOOLS TO OWN OR RENT:

BUILDER'S LEVEL; CONCRETE-FINISHING TOOLS; PORTABLE CIRCULAR SAW; CORDLESS DRILL/DRIVER; RECIPROCATING SAW; TILE CUTTER OR TILE SAW.

MATERIALS YOU'LL NEED:

FORM LUMBER; READY-MIX CONCRETE; FRAMING LUMBER (SOME PRESSURE-TREATED); EXTERIOR-GRADE PLYWOOD SHEATHING; BUILDER'S FELT; ROOF SHINGLES; LATH/MESH FOR STUCCO; BACKER BOARD; THINSET MORTAR; TILE; TILE GROUT; GAS/WATER PIPE; ELECTRICAL CONDUIT.

PROJECT 10
A BASIC BUILT-IN

I t's not always the dramatic gesture that saves the day. The tried and true, however simple, most often leads to success, and this no-frills built-in grilling station offers an example.

Tied to a basic masonry wall and finished with stucco, this cooking center shares the same concrete block construction as its surroundings. It isn't grand in scale, elaborate in its detailing, or bristling with exotic materials. But it's a great facility that's easy to build and maintain.

The brick countertop is a no-fuss surface that can be fitted with a portable cutting board or a large serving tray. Veggies and side dishes can simmer on the gas burner while the rotisserie-equipped grill handles meat, fish, or fowl. Below, stainless-steel drawers offer storage for cooking accessories.

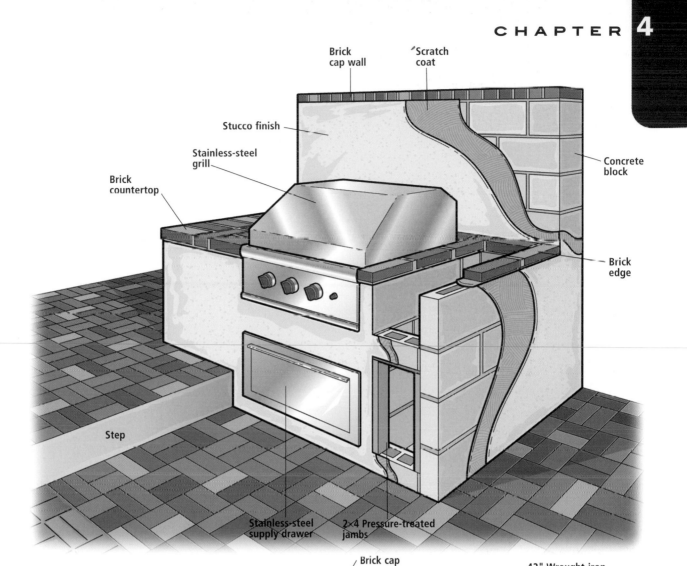

Brick cap wall

Scratch coat

Stucco finish

Stainless-steel grill

Brick countertop

Concrete block

Brick edge

Step

Stainless-steel supply drawer

2×4 Pressure-treated jambs

■ With a Mediterranean-style home and a brick courtyard establishing the theme, this outdoor kitchen doesn't stray far from its roots. But the simple look doesn't mean being shortchanged on function. There's a work counter, a built-in gas grill, a side burner, and drawer space for storage. Keeping the scale modest and tying to the existing wall saves significantly on costs and lets the cooking center mix seamlessly into the patio.

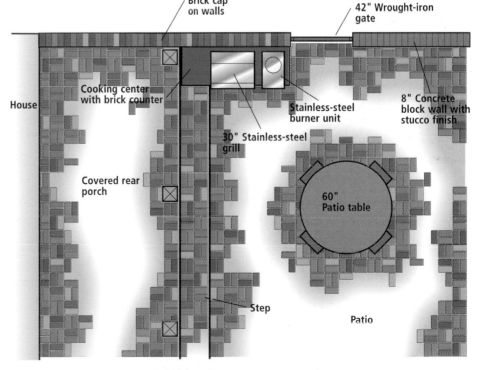

Brick cap on walls

42" Wrought-iron gate

House

Cooking center with brick counter

Stainless-steel burner unit

8" Concrete block wall with stucco finish

30" Stainless-steel grill

Covered rear porch

60" Patio table

Step

Patio

Porch, step, and patio are surfaced with brick pavers (basket-weave pattern)

■ Construction is simple and straightforward, thanks to the modular nature of the brick and block components.

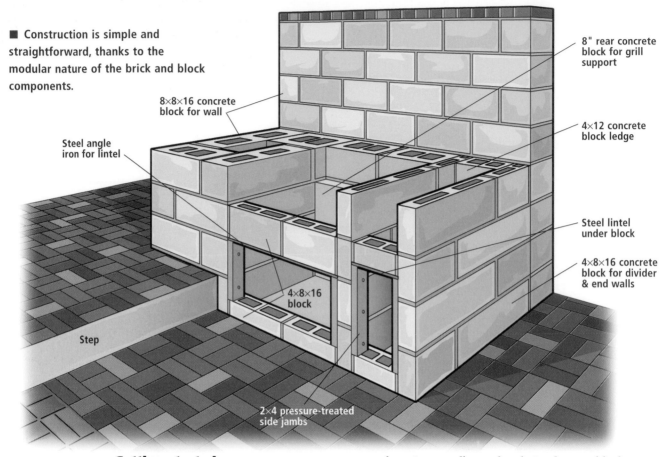

8×8×16 concrete block for wall

Steel angle iron for lintel

4×8×16 block

Step

2×4 pressure-treated side jambs

8" rear concrete block for grill support

4×12 concrete block ledge

Steel lintel under block

4×8×16 concrete block for divider & end walls

Getting started

The masonry wall and patio are essential elements in this design. The wall (see page 126) should be built before work on the cooking center begins; the brick patio (see page 124) can come later. This masonry project requires some foundation work—a trenched concrete footing for the wall and excavation for the patio.

The brick basket-weave pattern used for the patio can be mortared on top of a concrete slab or set in a sand base. In either case, excavate the topsoil to about a foot below the patio's finished level, then add a thick bed of crushed rock. Compact the rock in two or three layers for a final thickness of about 8 or 9 inches, then add a 2-inch layer of sand and set the bricks. If you are mortaring the brick, you'll need a 4-inch slab.

Support the block walls for the cooking center on a concrete slab or footing. In this case

the privacy wall was already in place, so blocks forming the rear wall of the cooking center were set against the wall and mortared together.

Mix the blocks

If you look closely at the illustration above, you can see different block sizes were used to create the desired wall thickness and proportions. For example, the rear wall base and closed (far) end of the cooking center use 8-inch-wide block, while the open front wall, the partition, and the near-end wall feature 4-inch-wide block. The narrower blocks offer plenty of strength but leave room for the side burner and grill. The top courses along the back of the cooking center are of narrower widths, creating a ledge below for the grill and burner housings. The construction of your kitchen will vary depending on the components you use, but using different block sizes is one way to create spaces of the right dimensions.

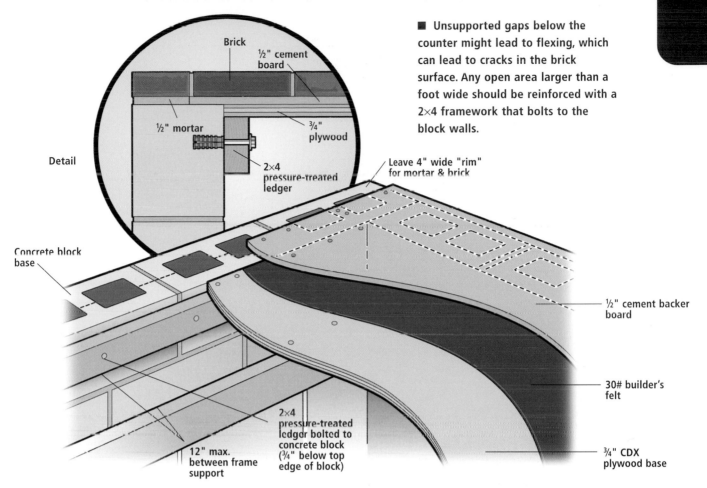

Detail

- Brick
- ½" cement board
- ½" mortar
- ¾" plywood
- 2×4 pressure-treated ledger

■ Unsupported gaps below the counter might lead to flexing, which can lead to cracks in the brick surface. Any open area larger than a foot wide should be reinforced with a 2×4 framework that bolts to the block walls.

Concrete block base

Leave 4" wide "rim" for mortar & brick

½" cement backer board

30# builder's felt

12" max. between frame support

2×4 pressure-treated ledger bolted to concrete block (¾" below top edge of block)

¾" CDX plywood base

Project sequence

A limited palette of materials keeps this project simple. Here's what you'll need to do, given an existing wall:

- Excavate and grade area for slab; run any underground utilities required.
- Set forms; add wire mesh or rebar.
- Pour and finish concrete slab; let cure a week.
- Mark cooking center layout and set first course of blocks.
- Set additional block courses; add pressure-treated side jambs for drawer bays and angle-iron lintels to support block above.
- Secure ledger blocks around openings where countertop will require support.
- Mount plywood inserts flush with top of surrounding block (above); cover inserts with builder's felt and backer board to within brick width of edges.
- Apply scratch and finish coats of stucco.
- Set bricks with mortar for countertop.
- Install grill, burner, and drawer units.

ESSENTIALS

PRIMARY SKILLS REQUIRED:

FORMING AND POURING A CONCRETE SLAB; LAYING CONCRETE BLOCK; BASIC CARPENTRY SKILLS; INSTALLING BRICK; BASIC PLUMBING SKILLS.

TOOLS TO OWN OR RENT:

BUILDER'S LEVEL; CONCRETE-FINISHING TOOLS; WET-CUTTING MASONRY/BRICK SAW; CORDLESS DRILL/DRIVER.

MATERIALS YOU'LL NEED:

FORM LUMBER; READY-MIX CONCRETE; EXTERIOR-GRADE ¾-INCH PLYWOOD; VARIOUS WIDTHS CONCRETE BLOCK (4-, 6-, AND 8-INCH WIDTHS); 2×4 PRESSURE-TREATED STOCK; ANGLE-IRON STOCK FOR LINTELS; BUILDER'S FELT; BACKERBOARD; THINSET MORTAR; GAS PIPE AND VALVE; STUCCO DRY MIX.

CONSTRUCTION BASICS

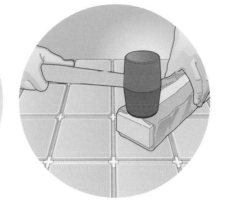
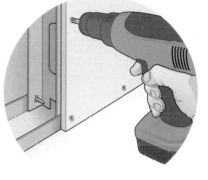

Building projects share a vocabulary of skills, tools, materials, and methods that can be mixed and matched to suit the job at hand. Whatever the particulars of the 10 outdoor kitchen projects featured in the previous chapter or any of the designs shown in other chapters, they each rely on this common language. Once you grasp the basic principles of construction, you can apply them to almost any project, adapting the designs to the specific requirements of your site.

Chapter 4 presents a "Project Sequence" for each kitchen. Each section includes a series of steps that precede any building activity, such as measuring and marking the site, excavating and grading the dirt, and setting forms for concrete footings or slabs. The stages proceed to placing and finishing concrete, installing prefabricated masonry products, such as brick or concrete block, or creating structures with a wood frame. This chapter provides detailed instructions to guide you successfully through these individual building techniques. Getting familiar with the tools, skills, and materials is the first step in planning the hands-on work required for your outdoor kitchen. Even if you choose to hire professionals for some or all of the construction, a working knowledge of these methods will help you hire the right people and communicate the kind of work you want done.

The techniques shown on the following pages have proven reliable and workable in most situations. They may not reflect regional differences or practices used by skilled tradespeople with specialized equipment. They may differ from code requirements in your area. Be sure to consult with your local building department before beginning any project.

WORKING WITH CONCRETE

Most outdoor kitchen projects involve concrete work. If you are fortunate enough to have a properly constructed slab already in place where you want to install a cooking center, the project almost certainly will progress faster and cost less. This can vary, however, depending on how elaborate your design is and whether it involves utility connections for water, electricity, and gas. Most utility lines will have to come through the slab floor of the kitchen, which might require cutting or drilling the concrete. In that case a surface layer of stone or ceramic tile might be necessary to camouflage the damage.

It's just as likely, though, that your project will require pouring a new slab. Like any permanent building feature, it will be subject to inspection by local building officials, so make sure you've submitted plans and received approval from the city or other governing body.

ANATOMY OF A CONCRETE SLAB

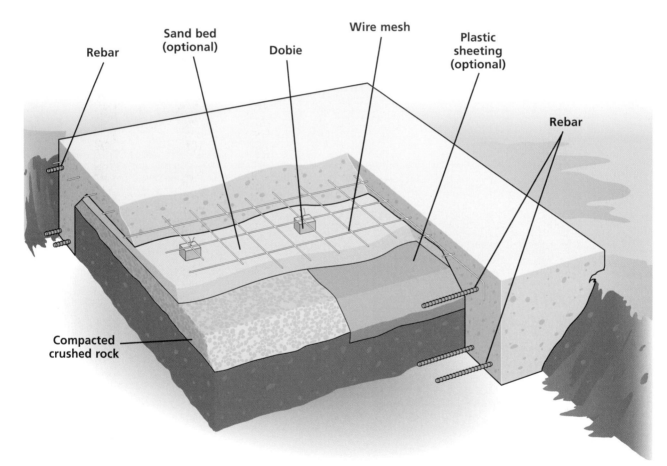

Rebar

Sand bed (optional)

Dobie

Wire mesh

Plastic sheeting (optional)

Rebar

Compacted crushed rock

◀ Concrete products typically come in dry, ready-to-mix versions. Use them only for small jobs. Order truck-mixed concrete for large projects.

In addition to structural considerations, such as slab thickness, the inspector will want to make sure you observe requirements for legal issues, such as minimum setbacks from property lines.

The chemical reactions that make concrete perform so well as a building material are complex, but working with the material is simple, at least for small residential projects. Once the concrete is mixed, the curing process is unstoppable, so you have to be ready to place and finish the material when it arrives. The stakes are high—if the few essential steps in the process aren't done properly, the slab will be weaker and subject to failures, such as cracking, surface crazing, and scaling. If the problems are bad enough, the slab will need to be broken up, removed, and repoured—an expensive and time-consuming job. Don't let these potential problems keep you from learning how to use a great building material. Just keep in mind that

WORK SAFELY

Wear safety glasses any time debris may fly, such as when cutting, hammering, or sanding. Use work gloves when handling materials or cleaning up, but not when using power tools (you might lose your grip). When working frequently with power tools, wear earplugs or earmuffs; in dusty conditions, wear a filter mask.

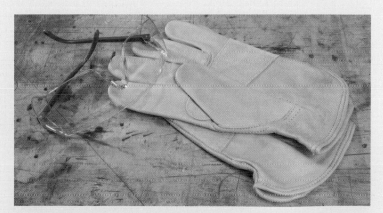

▲ Gloves and safety glasses should be part of your basic gear. Don't leave them in the toolbox—wear them!

concrete rewards preparation and patience but is unforgiving of carelessness.

Concrete basics

Concrete is a mixture of large and small aggregate (rock and sand, respectively) and portland cement, which is made by burning and grinding limestone and other ingredients into a fine powder. When water is added, a chemical reaction called hydration occurs, forming crystals in the cement and bonding the ingredients together. The rock (typically ¾ to 1 inch in diameter) and sand add body to the wet mix, provide surface to which the cement crystals adhere, and reduce the cost of the material by occupying volume.

Properly mixing concrete results in the aggregate and cement being suspended and distributed evenly throughout the material. After it's placed, the wet mix may be vibrated, tamped, or floated to bed the aggregate and eliminate air pockets or other voids. After the bleed water on the surface has dissipated, a

finish can be applied to the concrete as desired. Temperature, mixture type, water content, and other factors will determine how quickly the concrete hardens. Hot, dry weather accelerates hardening; cool or damp weather slows it down.

You can use dry, packaged ready-mix concrete for many small projects, but an 80-pound bag yields only ⅔ cubic foot of concrete mix. (See page 116 for more about calculating concrete volume.) Most patio slabs will require at least a couple of cubic yards of concrete, so even if you use a powered portable mixer, this isn't really an efficient or cost-effective way to buy the material. Your best bet will be to order the concrete from a ready-mix company and have it trucked, already mixed with rock, sand, and water, to the site. Most suppliers will help you determine the quantity and the kind of mix you need for your project, but it will help if you know something about the working properties of the material.

■ The strength of concrete lies in its ability to withstand compression; it is relatively weak against tension (pulling or bending forces). For a slab to last, it has to be well supported under its entire area. Replacing topsoil with crushed rock or a similar aggregate, then compacting the bed with a vibrating plate compactor will help reduce settling underneath the slab and decrease the likelihood of cracking. Steel reinforcing rod (rebar) or wire mesh is used to prevent separation if cracks occur.

■ Sturdy forms built from 2× lumber (or an equivalent material) are

▼ Troweling a concrete slab has to be done after the bleed water dissipates but before the mix sets too firmly. The steel edge compresses the surface and reduces porosity.

CONCRETE FINISHING TOOLS

required to contain the wet concrete, which can exert tremendous force when placed. Support stakes should be no more than 2 feet apart. If a form gives way during the pour, it will be almost impossible to reset it accurately with the concrete still in place. The recommended minimum thickness for a residential slab is typically about 4 inches in the center, with a slight taper to a thicker edge at the perimeter. Use 2×6 framing lumber to build forms for a slab. If you want thicker edges, the surrounding soil below the forms can act as a natural dam for the concrete.

■ Clean water is a necessary ingredient, but too much in the mix will result in larger gaps between cement crystals, creating a weaker slab, even when it is fully cured. Too little water will shorten the hydration process and make the mix harder to place and finish. The stiffness and consistency of the mix can be measured with a slump test, which registers the amount of settling it undergoes when a 12-inch test cone is removed. A low slump indicates a stiff mix (one that doesn't settle much); a high slump means the mix flows readily and may be too wet. All you need to keep in mind is that a 5- to 6-inch slump is typical for an exterior slab.

■ Air entrainment is a common method for making concrete less susceptible to freeze damage in cold environments. Special admixtures trigger chemical reactions that produce oxygen. The resulting air bubbles leave microscopic voids that allow for the expansion of freezing water in the concrete, relieving stresses that might crack the slab. Typical mix for residential slabs is around 6 percent; ask a

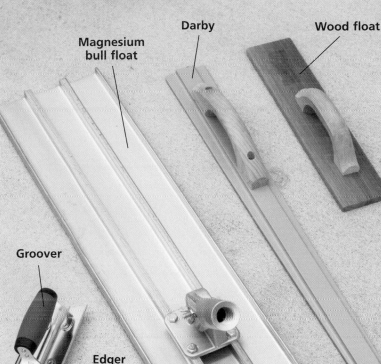

Magnesium bull float

Darby

Wood float

Groover

Edger

Pointed trowel

Trowel

local concrete supplier for details and common entrainment treatments in your area.

■ Admixtures are chemical additives used to reduce water content, retard or speed curing, or compensate for certain site or climatic conditions. For most residential jobs they aren't necessary, but ask your supplier or concrete contractor before ordering.

■ Control joints are thin cuts or grooves in the concrete surface with a depth of about one-fourth the thickness of the slab. They're used to prevent a slab from cracking randomly, either from shrinkage stresses during the curing process or from later stresses, such as frost heaving. They provide a preweakened line where a crack can form without being visible at the surface. The joint can be hand-tooled in wet concrete using a groover or sawn in a fresh slab once it sets up firmly enough (usually within 24 hours of the pour).

■ Proper curing is one of the most critical factors in producing durable concrete. This means that after floating the slab to seat the rock aggregate and troweling to consolidate the surface, you want to keep the concrete from drying out too quickly. Cement crystals continue to form only in the presence of water, so after troweling and finishing the surfaces, use a spray-on curing compound or plastic sheeting to cover the slab. Allow at least three days–preferably a week–before uncovering or working on the slab (unless it's to cut control joints).

CALULATING CONCRETE VOLUME IN A SLAB

When you order ready-mix concrete, specify the quantity in cubic yards, which measure 3 feet in each dimension for a volume total of 27 cubic feet ($3\times3\times3=27$). To determine the volume in a slab, multiply the length times the width times the thickness. All dimensions should be recorded in feet or fractions of a foot, not in inches.

For example, a slab measuring 10 feet wide by 16 feet long by 4 inches thick ($\frac{1}{3}$ foot) would set up the following equation: $10\times16\times\frac{1}{3}=53.3$ cubic feet, or just under 2 cubic yards. If the slab shape is not a rectangle or square, sketch it and divide it into simpler shapes. Then calculate the volume of each section and total those figures.

In most cases allow a margin of at least 10 percent extra to make sure you have enough concrete ordered. If you have any left over, you can use it to pour a small pad, sidewalk section, or stepping stones. (Prepare for the possibility ahead of time by setting up forms.) If the nature of the design makes it too difficult to estimate the concrete volume accurately, check in your area for a ready-mix provider with trucks that measure and mix the concrete on-site. It's slightly more expensive per yard than conventional ready-mix, but you pay only for what you use.

USING REINFORCING STEEL

Because concrete can crack from stresses caused by shrinkage or inadequate substrate support, reinforcing steel is often used to control such damage. In many cases steel cannot prevent the formation of cracks, but it can often limit the damage by keeping the concrete subsequently from shifting and widening the cracks. Your local building officials are likely to have specific requirements for the type, size, and placement of reinforcing steel in concrete structures, so check with them as you draw your plans.

■ Light- or medium-duty slabs are often reinforced with sheets of steel wire mesh that feature a grid of 6-inch square openings The effectiveness of the mesh depends on its proper placement in the concrete. For best results it should be within about 2 inches of the surface, which often doesn't occur when it is placed on the bare ground and simply pulled up into the concrete as the slab is poured. The preferred method is to place and strike off about half the concrete thickness, lay the mesh, then pour the remaining concrete. Another common technique is to tie the wire mesh in place before the pour, supported by small concrete blocks called chairs or dobies. When the concrete is poured it flows under and around the mesh. (Note: Don't use brick for these chairs; it's too absorbent and may lead to excess moisture and cracking.)

■ Heavier reinforcement can be achieved using a textured steel reinforcing rod, commonly called rebar. It is typically sold in 20-foot lengths (some home centers carry 10-foot lengths) and is labeled according to its diameter as expressed in eighths of an inch. For example, #3 rebar is $\frac{3}{8}$ inch in diameter, and #4 rebar is $\frac{1}{2}$ inch ($\frac{4}{8}$) in diameter. Though the material comes in much larger diameters, these two sizes are fine for most residential work and can be easily cut and bent with common tools. Like wire mesh, rebar can be set into wet concrete or placed on supports before the concrete is poured. Overlapped ends must be wired together, and you should always allow at least 3 inches of coverage from the concrete surfaces. In slabs rebar can be laid around the perimeter of the area, where the concrete is thicker.

■ Be aware that some contractors consider using reinforcing steel in small residential slabs unnecessary. Some use fiber-reinforced concrete mixes (with tiny pieces of fiberglass dispersed throughout the mix). Some reinforcement, however, is recommended so cracks that might form don't worsen over time, and local codes may require it.

▼ Reinforcing steel increases concrete's resistance to breakage and prevents separation of the concrete if cracks occur.

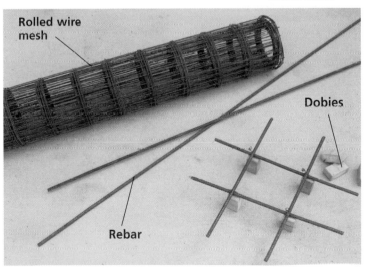

Rolled wire mesh

Dobies

Rebar

POURING A SLAB

Even in mild climates where freezing soil is of little or no concern, most slabs will fare better if you remove the topsoil and replace it with a bed of compacted crushed rock and a compacted layer of sand. This will help prevent unwanted settling and cracking, and if temperatures drop and stay below freezing, the improved drainage underneath the slab will make frost heaving and other water-related problems less likely.

You can hire a grading and excavating contractor to remove the soil with a skid loader, but unless the slab area is exceptionally large (more than 250 square feet), you can save the expense and dig it yourself. Still, hand-digging can be slow, difficult work. Consider renting a rototiller to break up the sod or soil. It's relatively inexpensive (typically $75–$100 per day), reasonably quick, and causes less collateral damage than a tractor in your backyard. It breaks up the topsoil so you can gather it easily

into a wheelbarrow and redistribute it elsewhere in the yard. Excavate enough soil to allow for a rock and/or sand base from 4 to 8 inches thick, plus the slab thickness. Don't rely on visual estimates for this; run string between batterboards at various locations so you can gauge the depth of the dig.

Here's an outline of the sequence you'll follow to pour a slab:

1 Use stakes, batterboards, and string to mark the outline, as shown in the illustration below. (This presumes the slab is square or rectangular. For curved or other irregular shapes, see page 121.)

2 Excavate the topsoil and replace it with a gravel and/or sand bed. Use a vibrating compactor (available from a rental center) to compress this material. The compaction can be done before and after forms are installed.

▶ **Batterboards and mason's lines allow the necessary adjustments when laying out a slab. Measuring for a 3-4-5 triangle ensures a 90-degree corner.**

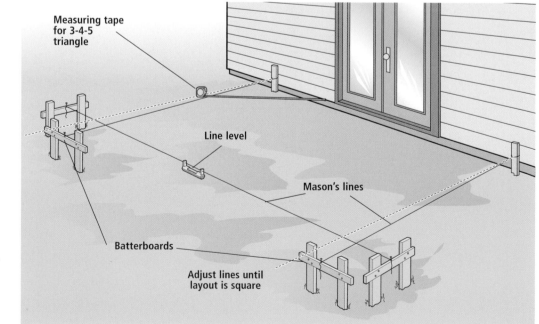

Measuring tape for 3-4-5 triangle

Line level

Mason's lines

Batterboards

Adjust lines until layout is square

❸ Set and brace the forms. You'll need to buy an inexpensive water level or rent a builder's transit to mark level lines on grade stakes. Run string to outline the edges of the forms so they're straight and level. Plastic sheeting can be placed over the substrate, either sandwiched between layers of sand and gravel or left exposed.

❹ Cut and fit the reinforcing steel you plan to use in the slab, either wire mesh or rebar. Tie it in place on support blocks or set it in place about halfway through the pour. Make sure at least 2 to 3 inches of concrete covers the steel.

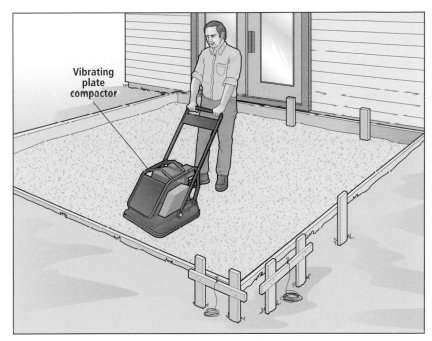

Vibrating plate compactor

▲ Compacting the crushed-rock base is critical to prevent settling of the slab. Add the rock in layers 4–8 inches thick and alternate the direction of the compactor.

POURING A CONCRETE SLAB

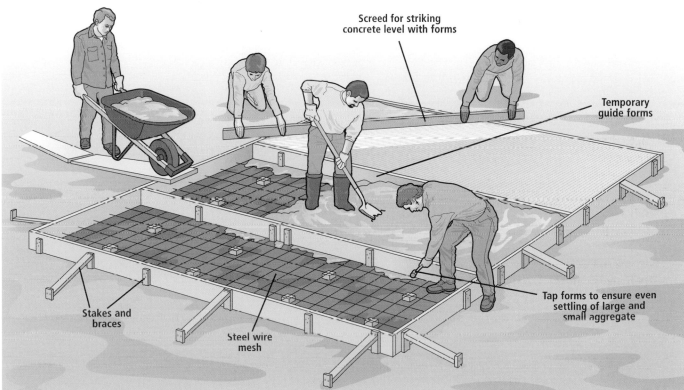

Screed for striking concrete level with forms

Temporary guide forms

Stakes and braces

Steel wire mesh

Tap forms to ensure even settling of large and small aggregate

POURING A SLAB (CONTINUED)

▶ A bull float is required for large slabs. It enables you to float the entire surface from outside the forms. Do this before the bleed water appears.

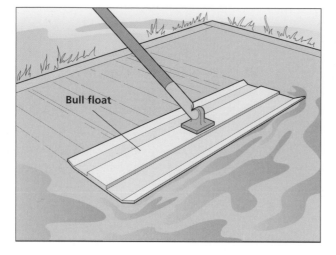

Bull float

▶ Use a groover and straightedge to form control joints in the wet concrete, unless you intend to cut them later with a saw. Rerun the tool after you trowel the slab.

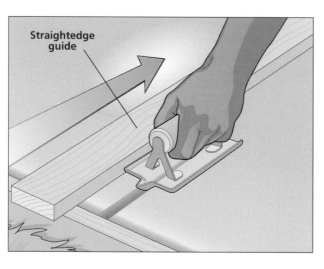

Straightedge guide

▶ After using a pointed trowel to dislodge any large aggregate along the form, run an edging tool to create a rounded contour along the edge of the slab.

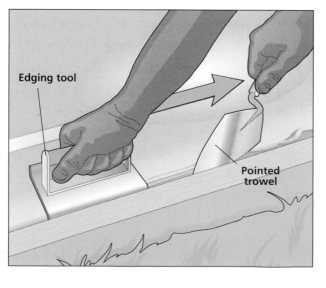

Edging tool

Pointed trowel

5 Have shovels, wheelbarrows, tools, and all your helpers ready, then call in the mixer truck. Dampen the substrate so it doesn't pull water out of the concrete mix too quickly. Then start the pour. If possible, get the chute directly into the area so you don't have to transport the concrete in batches. Keep the chute end low and moving to distribute the concrete evenly. For large slabs pour sections and strike them off as you work, but always keep the working edge moving. If you stop partway and restart, the concrete may form a cold joint where it doesn't bond properly.

6 Use a straight 2×4 or other board as a screed to strike off and level the concrete with the top edges of the forms. A first pass with a tamping motion will help settle any large aggregate that's too close to the surface. Then slide the screed along the forms with a slight side-to-side sawing motion. Fill in any low spots, then run the screed again until the surface is flat and level.

7 The next step is called floating, which must be done before the bleed water appears on the surface. Floating forces large aggregate down and consolidates the surface. On small areas use a hand float or darby. Wood is the traditional material, but magnesium is better for air-entrained concrete. On large slabs use a bull float, which is longer and has a handle like a broom. Keep the leading edge of the float slightly elevated and drag the tool across the concrete. For best results make the first float pass perpendicular to the strike-off direction; make a second pass perpendicular to the first.

8 If you're including control joints, rough them out now using a groover and a straightedge. Also use a pointed trowel to score along the edges of the forms (to displace the aggregate), then run an edger along the perimeter of the slab. This creates a slightly rounded edge that's less prone to chipping or causing injury. (You'll repeat these tasks later.)

POURING CURVED OR IRREGULARLY SHAPED SLABS

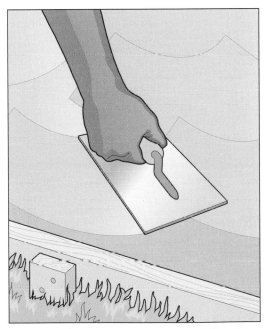

▲ **Use arc-like motions as you trowel the slab. Hold the leading edge of the trowel up slightly so it doesn't catch and gouge the surface.**

Curved shapes require slightly different preparation. Use garden hoses or rope to create the shape on the ground; then mark the outline with sand. Forms should be made from thin, flexible wood and must be built up in layers. Use extra stakes and braces for support. You may also backfill with dirt along the form for additional support. The same techniques for leveling the forms apply. The sequence for placing and finishing the concrete is the same as described on the preceding pages.

POURING A SLAB (CONTINUED)

9 Wait for the bleed water to dissipate before troweling. If you're not sure about the timing, step onto the slab with one foot. If the concrete is ready to trowel, your weight will leave an impression about ¼ inch deep. Do not add water, dry cement powder, or anything else to the concrete at this stage; doing so will likely cause surface failures later.

10 Using knee boards (made of plywood or rigid foam) to support your weight, start troweling the slab. This process compacts and hardens the surface and makes it smoother. Work in wide, sweeping arcs, always keeping the leading edge of the trowel slightly elevated. Two or three passes are sufficient.

11 Make follow-up passes on control joints and edges to clean them, then touch up any affected areas with a trowel. Drag a push broom lightly across the slab to give it a slight texture. (This step is optional but recommended for exterior applications such as a patio, which should have a nonslip surface.)

12 The concrete now needs to cure—this final step is critical to its strength. This process requires water, proper temperature, and time; the first few days are especially crucial. Covering the slab with plastic helps keep moisture in but may cause slight marking or discoloration on the surface. Alternate methods include using spray-on curing compounds, covering the slab with wet burlap, or tossing loose straw onto the slab and keeping it damp. For small slabs you can use a misting spray head (available at masonry supply centers) attached to a garden hose to keep the slab moist. Repeated cycles of wetting and drying the surface are hard on the concrete, so don't let it dry out during this initial period.

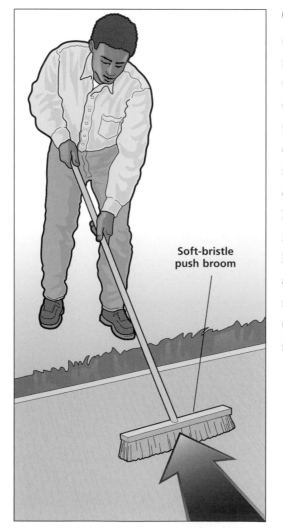

Soft-bristle push broom

▶ Adding a broom texture is the simplest way to create a nonslip surface in concrete. Let the weight of the broom head do the work; pull in a straight line toward you.

BRICK PAVER PATIOS

Building a patio with bricks or other pavers involves many of the same preliminary steps you'd use for a concrete slab. The site needs to be excavated and graded level, and a compacted bed of crushed rock should replace the topsoil. From that point on the construction techniques differ.

1 Establish the perimeter of the patio so the brick is contained and doesn't shift. This can be done with permanent forms made of pressure-treated wood, poured concrete curbs, or with edging bricks, called soldiers, set vertically into the ground. Set the edging straight and level, just like a concrete form, because it will function as a guide for laying the field bricks.

2 The base of crushed rock provides drainage. A layer of bedding sand makes it much easier to fine-tune the position of the bricks as you lay them. Typically an inch of sand is adequate for brick patios. Once the edging is installed, add the sand and spread it evenly with a rake or push broom. If you've rented a vibrating compactor, make a couple of passes to consolidate the sand, then add more as needed to bring the layer to the approximate height needed.

3 Make an offset screed to strike the sand to a consistent level (see illustration below). Technically the offset should be equivalent to the thickness of the bricks so that when they are

▼ Once you've established secure edges for the brick area with forms or soldier bricks, add sand and use an offset screed to strike it off at the desired level. Gauge the offset so when the brick settles (as much as ½ inch when vibrated), it will be the finish height you want.

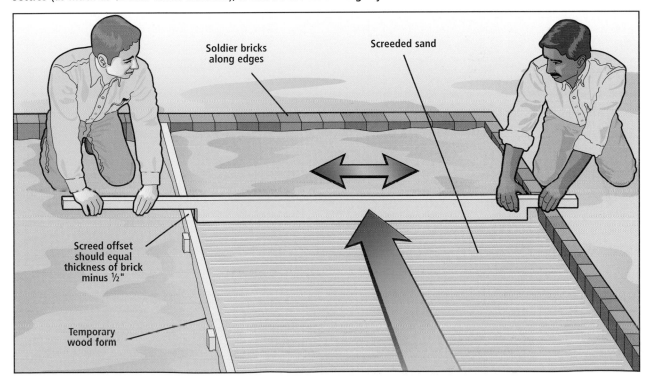

Soldier bricks along edges

Screeded sand

Screed offset should equal thickness of brick minus ½"

Temporary wood form

BRICK PAVER PATIOS (CONTINUED)

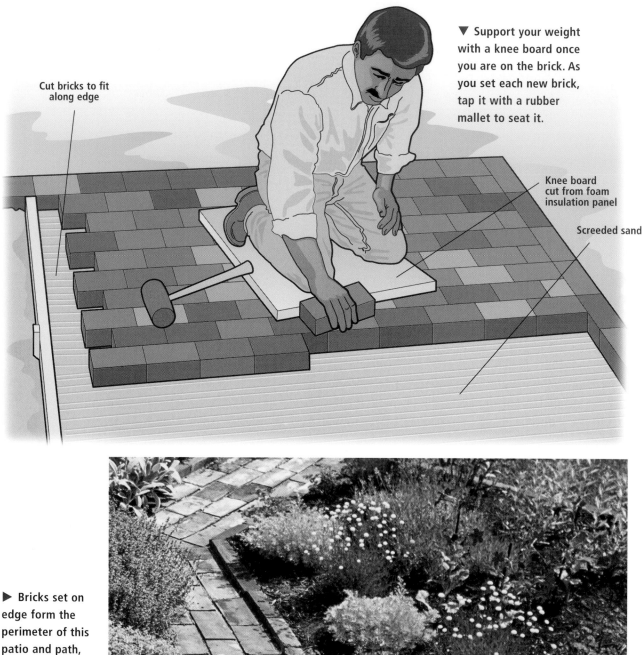

Cut bricks to fit along edge

▼ Support your weight with a knee board once you are on the brick. As you set each new brick, tap it with a rubber mallet to seat it.

Knee board cut from foam insulation panel

Screeded sand

▶ Bricks set on edge form the perimeter of this patio and path, serving both to provide a visual transition to the landscaping and to hold the field bricks in place.

installed, their upper faces are flush with the top of the edging. Some settling is likely to occur, however, so if you don't want the brick surface to end up lower than the edges, reduce the offset on the screed slightly. The amount of settling is hard to predict, but if you lay the brick raised about ¼ to ½ inch above the edging and vibrate it with a compactor, it should settle to the approximate height you want.

4 Place all of the bricks, then sweep sand over the surface to fill the joints. If you run a

compactor on the bricks, use duct tape to secure a carpet remnant or other cushion to the bottom so the metal plate on the machine doesn't crack the bricks. Make several passes over the entire area, alternating directions as you work.

5 Once you're confident that all the bricks are properly seated, use a garden hose to wet down the surface and further consolidate the sand in the joints. Add sand to fill as needed.

BRICK PATTERNS

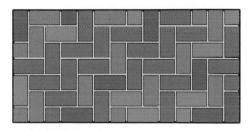

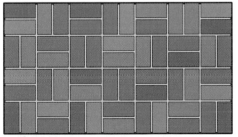

Running bond

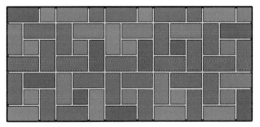

Basket weave with borders

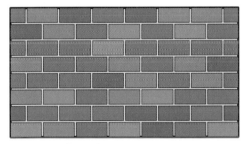

Basket weave

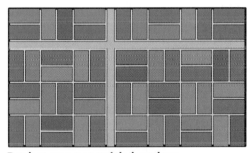

Pinwheel

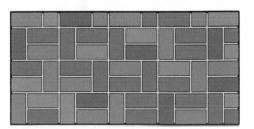

Half-basket weave

Herringbone

UILDING CONCRETE BLOCK WALLS

Though brick and stone veneers are the most common exterior surfaces for masonry walls, concrete block routinely provides the underlying structure. It's inexpensive and durable, and its large unit size (a full block typically measures 8×8×16 inches) allows for quick and efficient building methods. Whether laid over a narrow concrete footing or directly on a concrete slab, a block-wall enclosure provides stable and durable support for an outdoor cooking center.

Be sure to use genuine concrete blocks rather than cinder blocks, which are less dense and more subject to damage from freezing and exposure. Care taken during the layout and planning stages will yield an easier construction process and better results. Take careful measurements for the block spacing and layout to establish the corners and lines of the walls.

▼ Concrete block is a modular material, so caps and half-units are offered to complete a project. Smaller pavers and bricks can be applied as accents or a veneer.

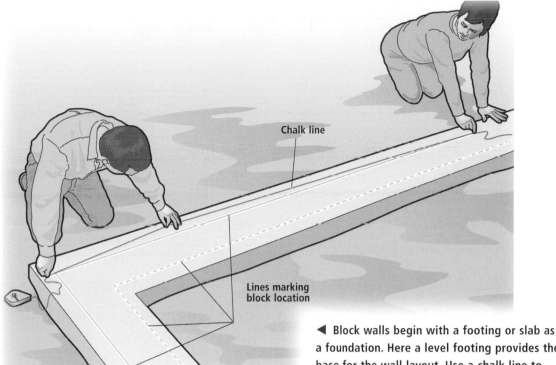

Chalk line

Lines marking
block location

◀ Block walls begin with a footing or slab as a foundation. Here a level footing provides the base for the wall layout. Use a chalk line to mark a guide for the first course of blocks.

Solid foundation

A block wall relies on a solid base foundation for support. The best option for this is a poured concrete footing reinforced with steel rebar.

1 Trench or excavate the soil to define the area for the footing. Try to plan wall lengths in multiples of 16 inches. If you can do this, you'll avoid having to cut blocks to fit.

2 Set forms for the footing just as you would for a concrete slab, using framing lumber and support stakes. Typically a footing should be at least twice as wide as the wall it will support and at least 8 to 10 inches thick. If the wall will be taller than a few feet or if it will hold back a slope, add vertical rebar stems every 16 or

▼ Use a mason's trowel to spread the mortar for the first course.

32 inches in the footing, spaced so they run through the open cells in the blocks.

3 After the footing is poured, do a dry run with the first course so you can check the block layout, then remove the block and snap chalk lines. Your layout stakes and other markers will make it easy to snap lines exactly along the block location, but as you place the mortar bed, the line will be covered. To keep a straight block line, tie mason's line on stakes to guide you, or snap additional offset chalk lines that will remain visible as you work.

4 Place the mortar bed between the lines. Concrete block is sized so a ⅜-inch-thick mortar joint brings the total height and length of a block to its nominal dimensions. Try to keep this consistent as you work. Lay the mortar bed about an inch thick and compress it firmly as you set blocks directly on top of the footing.

5 Set the first course of blocks. If you look closely, you'll notice that a block has wider edges (and smaller cell openings) on one face. This results from the way blocks are formed in the mold. Set the block with the wide edges up.

▶ With chalk lines snapped, set the first block in a corner. You can mark guide lines for the exact placement of the block or allow for an offset so the lines stay visible after the mortar is placed on the footing.

Chalk line

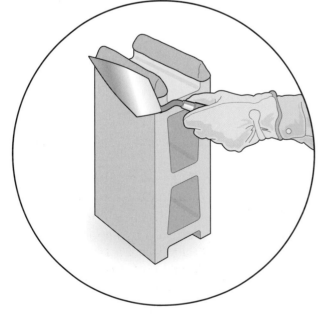

◀ With each subsequent block, "butter" the end that will face the block just installed. Excess mortar will squeeze out as the block is set; it can be scraped off and reused.

► Accurately set mason's lines will speed work up, but you should also check with a level to ensure proper alignment of the blocks. Even the first course must be checked for consistent thickness of the mortar bed.

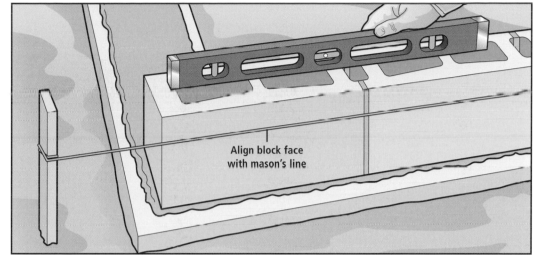

Align block face
with mason's line

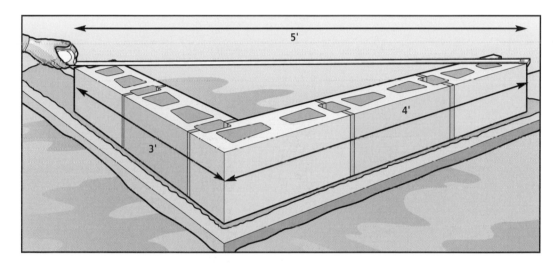

5'

4'

3'

◄ Use the 3-4-5 method to check the corner for square. Measure 3 feet from the corner on one side; 4 feet on the other. If the corner is square, the length between the points will measure 5 feet.

◄ Build lead corners first by placing several courses of block at each corner. Tie a guide line to help align the field blocks as you add them.

6 For the remaining courses, trowel the mortar on about ¾ inch thick, then compress it as you place the block. Use story poles and guide strings at the lead corners to ensure the correct course heights as the wall goes up.

7 Plan each course so that the final block, the closer, is a full block. Butter both ends and the adjoining blocks and slide the closer in carefully. If the mortar is scraped off as you place it, remove it, butter it again and replace it.

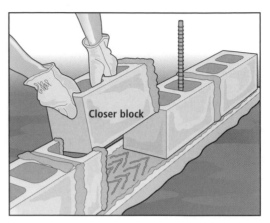

▲ Finish each course with a full closer block.

ADDING STEEL REINFORCEMENT

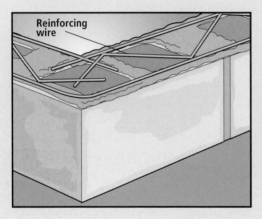

◄ Mortar and concrete are extremely strong in compression but are not flexible. If the ground settles, freezes and thaws, or exerts lateral pressure, cracks may develop. Wire reinforcement helps keep cracks from forming or spreading.

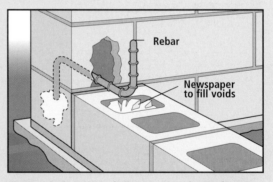

▲ Joints between two wall sections can be reinforced with short lengths of steel reinforcing rod (called rebar), bent in a Z shape. (Use ⅜-inch diameter rebar; it's plenty strong for this and easier to bend.) Fill in with concrete.

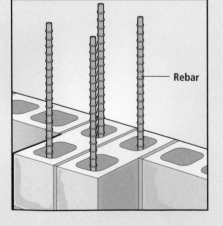

◄ Tall walls or columns, especially those that must withstand lateral pressure, should be reinforced with vertical lengths of steel rebar. When all the blocks have been set, fill the cavities with concrete so the steel is completely embedded.

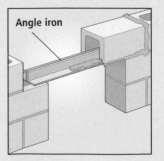

◄ Angle iron adds the span strength needed for lintels, which bridge gaps created for access openings. Special U-shape blocks are used on the lintel.

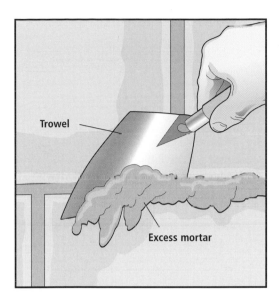

Trowel

Excess mortar

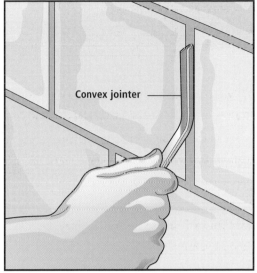

Convex jointer

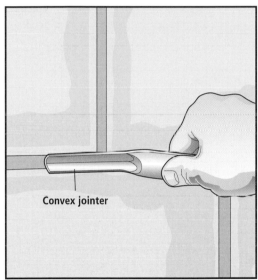

Convex jointer

■ Tooling the mortar joints has to be done periodically as you build the wall. Scrape the excess away with a trowel shortly after you place each block and keep building while the mortar starts to set. Strike the vertical joints first with a convex jointer, then the horizontal. Make at least two passes as the joints firm up, then brush clean. Temperature, humidity, and the moisture content of the mortar and blocks will affect the set rate.

MORTARLESS BLOCK

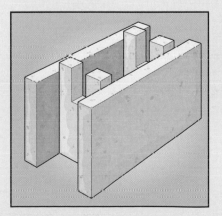

Here's an alternative to a conventionally mortared block wall. Self-aligning mortarless blocks feature interlocking contours and can simply be stacked on top of one another, then surfaced with a fiber-reinforced mortar. If it's a retaining wall or a similar installation where the wall structure will have to withstand substantial loads, steel rebar is laid between each layer, and the interior cavities in the block are filled with concrete or grout. Even without the exterior mortar, this added reinforcement makes interlocking block walls stronger than conventional ones.

Building Concrete Block Walls (CONTINUED)

Applying Stucco to Concrete Block

Applying stucco is a quick and inexpensive treatment that provides a decorative surface for concrete block walls. The material is a type of mortar troweled on in two or three layers. It can be colored with pigment or painted, and because it's hand-tooled, you can create a variety of textures on its surface. After applying a concrete-bonding agent to the block and letting it dry, trowel on the first layer (called the scratch coat) to a thickness ranging from ¼ to ½ inch. While it's still wet and pliable, rake the stucco with a small hand tool called a scarifier to create ridges on the surface (grooves about ⅛" deep). This gives the surface "tooth" to better hold the next layer.

For the best results let the scratch coat harden slightly and then apply another layer. This intermediate layer, called the brown coat, is optional, but its application makes the stucco more durable. You can rake this coat or leave the troweled finish. Whether one or two layers, the base coat of stucco should be kept moist and allowed to cure for a day or two.

Finally apply a ¼-inch finish coat of stucco and trowel it thoroughly. If you want to add texture, work a broom or brush over the finish coat, or spatter on a thin, spotty layer of stucco and knock the high spots down with a trowel. Allow the stucco to cure at least several weeks before painting.

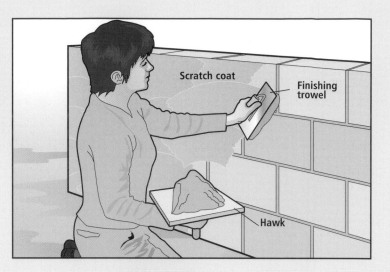

Scratch coat

Finishing trowel

Hawk

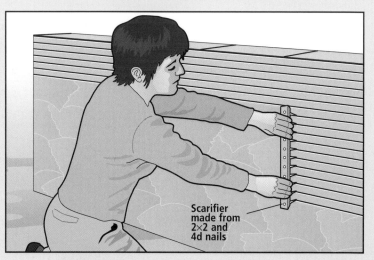

Scarifier made from 2×2 and 4d nails

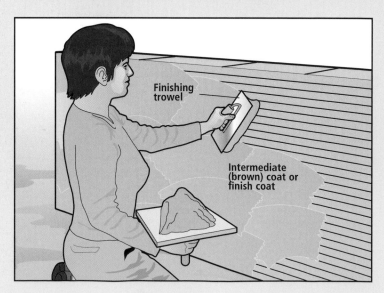

Finishing trowel

Intermediate (brown) coat or finish coat

ADDING BRICK OR STONE VENEER

It is possible to buy concrete blocks that have a textured, split, or decorative face. If you go that route, don't worry about adding any other surface material or treatment to the block walls. Many outdoor kitchen designs, however, feature a structural base of utility-grade concrete block that's surfaced with brick or stone veneer.

When brick veneer is applied to the exterior walls of a wood-frame house, a mason will typically leave a small airspace behind the brick. This gap helps insulate the wall and allows for drainage and ventilation to prevent moisture damage. Such precautions are usually unnecessary on a block-wall island for an outdoor kitchen. The application of a latex masonry bonding agent to the block surface allows the brick to adhere directly to the concrete block with mortar. Corrugated metal reinforcing ties, fastened to the block and bedded in the wet mortar of the brick joints, help secure the two layers together. The brick needs just as much support underneath as the structural block, so the first course should be bedded similarly on the slab or supported by a sturdy ledge. If the base of the wall is below grade, use 12-inch-wide block for the foundation course(s) and 8-inch-wide block above. That will leave a 4-inch ledge for the brick.

Manufactured stone veneer, made from portland cement mixed with lightweight aggregates, looks authentic but is much easier to work with than natural stone. It weighs far less and comes in convenient L-shape corner pieces that you won't find in nature. Its light weight keeps freight charges low, so its cost is competitive with natural stone. Stone veneer is applied using methods similar to brick veneer. Thin veneer, however, does not create the mortar-joint depth needed for metal brick ties.

Whatever veneer you choose, calculate the extra wall thickness into your plans so you have adequate overhang for countertops, plus proper depths and clearance for other features such as the grill or an undercounter appliance.

▶ The random shapes of stone or manufactured stone veneer let you place the pieces freehand, but pay attention to the overall balance as you work so you get a mix of size, shape, and color throughout.

Mortar scratch coat

Second mortar coat

BUILDING BRICK WALLS

Most brick structures, including cooking centers for outdoor kitchens, are built using brick as the finish surface over another structural component such as concrete block. However, it isn't necessary always to build this way with brick. Smaller projects such as planter walls can be built using just single-brick construction with no backing surface. Candidates for this method include any nonloaded walls less than 2 feet tall. For taller walls or those that have to shoulder more of a structural load, you can build a wall two bricks deep so each layer provides lateral support for the other. On alternating courses (as many as five courses apart), a row of bricks is laid perpendicular to the others. You can also bed layers of steel mesh in the mortar joints for additional reinforcement. However, this double-

▶ Laying brick is a repetitive task, so you'll get better results if you can get a rhythm going. Use a throwing motion to place the mortar, then follow up with a quick side scrape to trim excess.

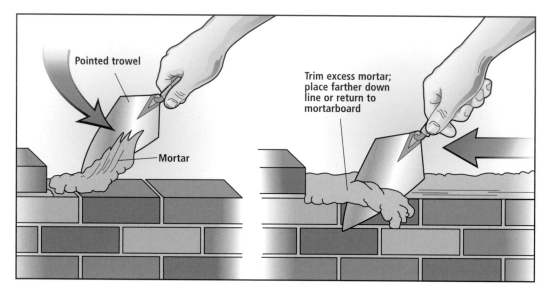

▶ Drag a pointed trowel to create a small trough in the mortar bed for uniform setting of the bricks. As you work, butter one end of the next brick with mortar so you don't have to fill the joint after the brick is set.

▲ Press the brick firmly enough to force excess mortar out of the joint. Trowel it off and keep moving. As the mortar starts to set, strike the joints.

wall-brick-only method is a slower and more expensive way to build, so it isn't as common.

Compared to more modern construction techniques, bricklaying seems like slow, plodding work. Watch a skilled mason, though, and you'll see how quickly a wall goes up. The reason? The repetition allows for a steady rhythm, so once you get going you can make good progress. In many ways, laying bricks is like setting concrete block. Here are some tips to make the job go smoothly:

■ To speed your work, set the materials within easy reach. Presoak a batch of bricks in water.

As you use them, replace with others. Use a mason's hawk to hold mortar at the ready.

■ With a brick trowel, toss the mortar onto the previous course, scrape off the excess, then drag the point of the trowel through the center of the mortar layer to sculpt a small trough. Butter the end of the next brick with mortar, place it, and scrape away excess mortar as it squeezes out.

■ Don't try to tool joints too soon. As with block joints, allow some time for the mortar to set before striking it off with a jointing tool. Meanwhile, place bricks along that course.

■ If you notice that the mortar becomes thin as

Straight 2×4 **Level**

▲ For small projects that don't warrant the building of lead corners, make constant checks to ensure that the brick courses are level. Even if the finished height will require only a few courses, check for plumb and square corners. Your eye is an unreliable judge when you're working close in.

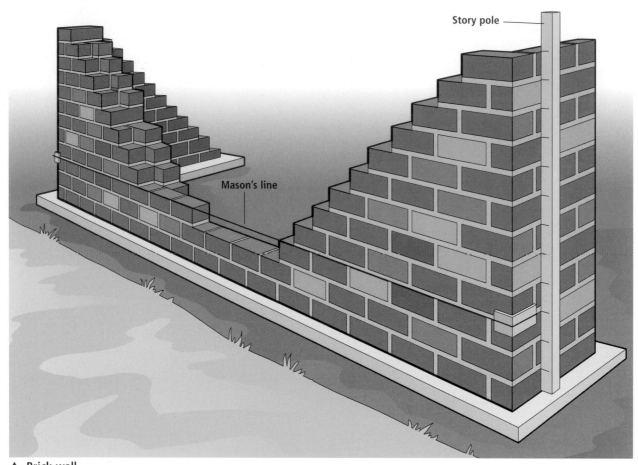

Story pole

Mason's line

▲ Brick wall construction follows the same principles as those used for concrete block. Make a story pole to achieve consistent course heights, build lead corners first, then use guide strings as you fill in the remaining wall.

you place each brick, your bricks are too wet. They should be damp so they don't wick the moisture too quickly from the mortar, which will result in a weak joint.

■ If getting consistent joint thickness seems difficult, check a masonry supply store for a mortaring guide or template. These simple tools, usually made of cast aluminum or injection-molded plastic, create a self-spacing pocket for the mortar as you place it. You set the tool on the previous course and butt it next to the brick just placed. The rim of the guide holds the mortar in and provides an automatic height gauge for the mortar (about ½ inch thick). They're a great help for DIYers.

■ As a general rule you can construct brick walls up to about 6 feet in length using just a builder's level and a straightedge. At that scale you can keep the bricks aligned as you work. If the wall is longer, use guide strings to help keep the rows straight. Work from the ends (or lead corners) toward the center.

■ If you're going more than six courses high, use a story pole so the course heights stay consistent. Stop periodically to strike the mortar with a jointing tool. Later dry brush the joints with a mason's brush.

■ Use water or a mild water-acid solution to remove the mortar residue from the brick faces.

BRICK AND BLOCK TRICKS OF THE TRADE

■ Calculate the layout ahead of time so you know how many bricks or blocks will fit in your assembly. Aim for overall dimensions that use full rather than cut units.

■ Even if you don't need to use lead corners for your masonry structure, drive a story pole (a stick marked with increments for each new course of block) at opposite ends so you can stretch a level line between them. Having a guide string improves speed and accuracy.

■ Wet, but don't soak, the surfaces that you're binding together with mortar. If they're bone dry, concrete and brick will wick the moisture out of the mortar before it can cure properly. If they're too wet, the excess moisture will dilute the mortar and reduce its strength.

■ Do periodic striking and tooling of the mortar joints as you work, not after you finish the entire wall area. On wall lengths under 12 feet, you can often set two or three courses before going back to strike and tool the joints. Temperature, humidity, and other conditions will affect the set rate of the mortar, so make repeat checks as you proceed. The mortar should be hardened enough to hold a tooled shape but still yield readily to firm pressure.

■ Just like concrete, mortar should cure slowly. Drape the wall with plastic sheeting when you finish so the wind and sun don't rob moisture from the joints.

■ Mineral residue from the mortar often creates a chalky discoloration on the brick called efflorescence. It will fade with time, but you can remove it immediately by washing the wall with a diluted muriatic acid solution (1 part acid to 10 parts water). This should be done within 24 hours of building the wall. (Safety note: Always add the acid to the water, never the water to the acid. Be sure to wear gloves and eye protection.)

▲ Existing brick walls with weakened mortar joints can have their structural integrity restored through a process called tuck pointing. Some of the old mortar is removed with a chisel or grinder, leaving shallow grooves between the bricks. A special tuck-pointing trowel is then used to press new mortar in place. It's time-consuming work but preferable to rebuilding the wall.

Working with Ceramic Tile

Ceramic tile ranks among the most commonplace and ancient of building materials, but it isn't just the legacy of tile that's enduring. Properly made and installed, tile provides a durable surface that can withstand heat, water, dirt, abrasion, modest impacts, direct sun, and just about any other hazard an outdoor environment presents. The key to such longevity lies in choosing the right tile for a given application, pairing it with the right substrate, and installing it correctly. (See "How to Mix Tile and Water" on page 143.)

Like brick, concrete, and other masonry products, tile has a split personality. Under compression (with weight bearing down on it), it

holds up well if given a solid support base. But it is rigid and doesn't flex without cracking, so it must have level, solid support. A typical countertop installation using ceramic tile begins with a substrate (the base upon which the tile is installed), which must provide two critical properties: good adhesion and rigidity. If the mortar or mastic can't adhere or the surface flexes under a load, the tile will break or work loose. Masonry substrates, such as concrete block or slab, are ideal, but other materials also work well if they are used properly. Tile showrooms stock and sell products for many different applications, so explain your intended use when you go shopping for materials.

With a masonry substrate, tile installation requires only a bed of thinset mortar, followed by grout for the joints. Many countertop projects, however, call for tile to be installed over a different substrate, usually a plywood or particleboard panel supported by a wood frame. In that case cement backerboard should be secured to the wood panel as the base for the mortar and tile.

Backerboard comes in ¼-inch and ½-inch thicknesses for residential use. It's basically a panel of compressed mortar reinforced with nylon or fiberglass mesh, beads of foam, or loose fibers embedded in the mix. It can be cut with a circular saw fitted with a carbide-tipped or diamond blade, or scored and snapped like wallboard. To fasten it to countertop bases or to wall studs, use special hardened screws. Finish the butted edges with mesh tape and trowel with thinset mortar. The techniques are virtually identical to those used for taping wallboard joints. The ½-inch-thick panels are the most common.

▲ Cement backerboard can be scored and snapped much like gypsum wallboard, but a carbide-tipped scoring tool is required for this abrasive material.

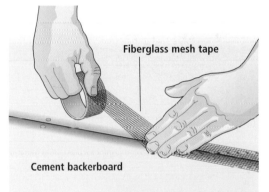

◀ After the backerboard panels have been secured with screws, use self-adhesive mesh tape to cover the indented seams.

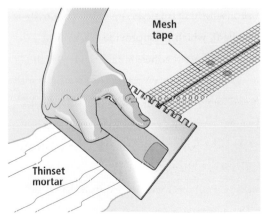

▲ Use a trowel to spread thinset mortar into the joints. You don't need to sand and repeat if you get a reasonably flat seam on the first try.

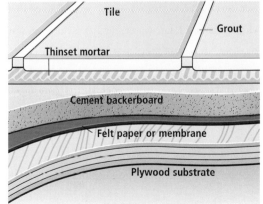

▲ A typical countertop installation builds on a wood base. A membrane adds waterproofing; backerboard provides stiffness for the tile.

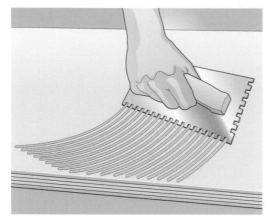

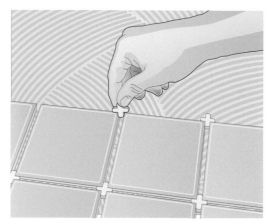

▲ Proper setting of tile requires a uniformly thick bed of mastic or thinset mortar. Use a notched trowel to ensure that the adhesive is spread to a consistent thickness. For tiles smaller than 6×6 inches, a ⅛-inch notch works best. Use a ¼-inch notch for larger tiles.

▲ Plastic spacers help you position the tile consistently. Seat the tiles with a mallet and padded block before the mortar hardens.

Notched trowels

Grout float

Snap cutter

Tile nippers

Rubber mallet with block

Setting tile

1 Once you've installed the cement backerboard and taped the seams, take some time to think through the tile layout. You want to start on a reference line in the middle of your tile area, positioned so the pattern looks good and so the cut tiles are balanced on either end of the area. Make layout decisions before setting the first tile; do a dry run with loose tile, then snap a chalk line to create a straight guide for installing the first row.

2 For field tiles (the standard-shape tiles used for most of the surface), the installation is simple

CUTTING TILE

▲ A snap cutter will etch a fine line in the glazed surface. Press the lever down to snap the tile along the line.

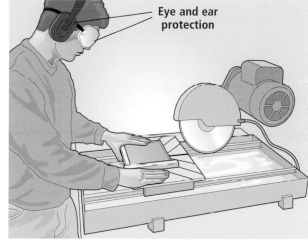

Eye and ear protection

▲ For thick tiles or angled cuts, nothing beats a wet-cutting tile saw with a diamond-studded blade. You can get one from most rental centers for less than $75 a day.

and straightforward. Apply thinset mortar with a notched trowel so the coverage is a consistent thickness. Spread only as much mortar as you can cover with tiles in a few minutes' time. Once the thinset starts to set up, it's difficult to achieve a consistent depth when you place the tiles.

3 Place the tile and tap it gently to seat it in the mortar. Some tiles have lugs along the edges and are self-spacing; with others you insert plastic spacers between the tiles to maintain a uniform gap.

4 Edges or obstacles will require cutting tile to fit. Simple cuts can be done with a scoring tool, which creates a line where the tile will break cleanly. A wet-cutting saw with a diamond blade takes less effort and offers more precision, plus it has the capacity to make partial or notched cuts. It's an expensive tool, but any well-equipped rental center will have one. For taking small pieces off the edge or corner of a tile, use nippers. This is a plier-like tool with two sharp

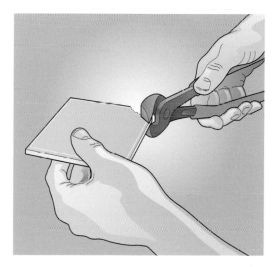

◀ Tile nippers are ideal for taking small bites from a tile and for tuning the contours of cuts made with a wet saw.

jaws that take controlled bites. It leaves a rough edge, so use it for cuts where an escutcheon or cover plate will camouflage the edge.

5 Transitions to other surfaces and edges will also involve specialty tiles that are formed to turn corners or accommodate a change in direction. These tiles are typically much more expensive than their matching field tiles, but fortunately you usually don't need very many. (see the illustration above).

Grouting tile

6 After all the tiles have been set, let the mortar cure overnight. The next day mix the grout to fill the joints. You can choose from a wide palette of colors to match, contrast, or complement the tile glaze. Light colored grout is the most common, but it's a poor choice for outdoor installations because it doesn't stay clean for long. Darker colors will hide the accumulation of dirt or stains much better.

7 Mix the grout to the recommended consistency, usually about the thickness of cake frosting. It should be stiff enough to hold its shape in the joints but still flow readily under pressure from the grout float. Use sweeping diagonal motions to bed the grout in the joints, changing directions occasionally to ensure full coverage.

8 When all the joints are full, wipe off the excess grout with a damp sponge. To get the tile clean, you'll have to rinse the sponge repeatedly in clean water as you work.

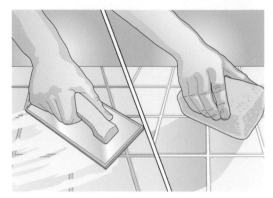

▲ Grout mix should be wet enough to flow into the tile joints but stiff enough to hold its shape. Work the float diagonally across the joints. Let the grout set, then sponge the tile clean with water.

9 Like other masonry products, grout benefits from a slow curing process. After wiping the tile clean, cover the countertop with clear plastic sheeting to keep wind and sun from stripping the moisture from the grout too quickly.

10 After allowing a few days for the grout to cure, clean the tile, apply a sealer to the entire surface, and wipe clean. The sealer won't affect the surface of a glazed tile, but porous materials, such as grout or unglazed tiles, will benefit from the added protection.

BACKSPLASH OPTIONS

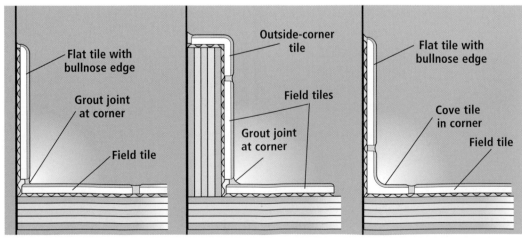

Flat tile with bullnose edge

Grout joint at corner

Field tile

Outside-corner tile

Field tiles

Grout joint at corner

Flat tile with bullnose edge

Cove tile in corner

Field tile

How to Mix Tile and Water

Even though glazed ceramic tile is considered a waterproof surface, there are differences in the material that make some tiles unsuitable for outdoor installations, especially where freeze-thaw cycles are likely to occur. Clay is naturally porous and will absorb some water, but variations in density and in firing conditions (the kiln temperature and duration of firing, for example) yield different kinds of tiles, some with a higher percentage of air pockets that can absorb water. Ask about the rating of the tile before you buy and select only vitreous or impervious tiles for use in an outdoor kitchen. Also plan on using a sealer on the grout once the tile has been grouted.

■ Nonvitreous—The water-absorption rate is as high as 7 percent (of tile weight). For decorative use only; use indoors or in dry locations.

■ Semivitreous—Fired slightly longer than nonvitreous tiles, semivitreous tiles have fewer air pockets and have a lower water absorption rate: between 3 and 7 percent. Use indoors only in dry or occasionally wet locations.

■ Vitreous—Fired at higher temperatures and for longer periods, vitreous tile has a higher density and a water absorption rate of less than 3 percent. Fine for outdoor use and in freezing environments but must be grouted.

■ Impervious—Fired twice as long as vitreous tile and at higher temperatures, impervious tile keeps water absorption limited to less than ½ percent. Not only are these tiles less susceptible to water damage, they are stronger and dense enough to thwart the growth of bacterial cultures, a welcome feature for countertops where food will be placed.

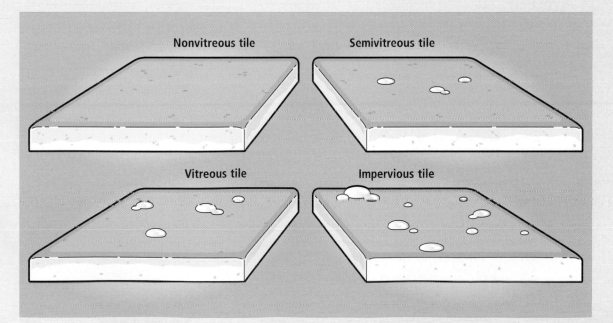

▲ This simple illustration depicts the differences in water absorption by various tile types. Nonvitreous tile is typically unglazed and soaks up any available moisture. The tile's glaze and density determine how effective it will be at repelling water and other liquids. Impervious tiles perform best and also resist freeze damage.

DECK-BUILDING BASICS

ANATOMY OF A DECK

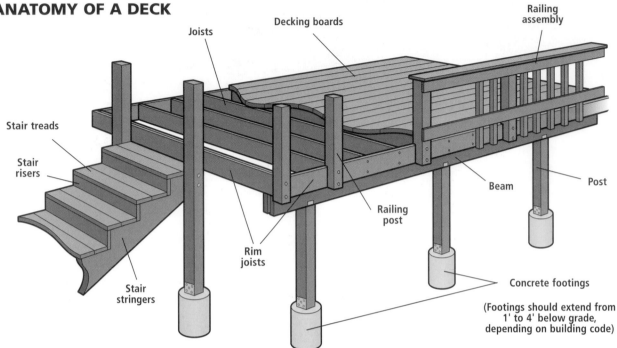

Joists

Decking boards

Railing assembly

Stair treads

Stair risers

Railing post

Rim joists

Stair stringers

Beam

Post

Concrete footings

(Footings should extend from 1' to 4' below grade, depending on building code)

A concrete or masonry patio is the most common setting for an outdoor kitchen, but some sites lend themselves better to a wood deck. It serves as the platform on which the kitchen is built or as a nearby setting for dining and entertaining.

Whether a deck is attached (tethered directly to the house) or freestanding, its primary structural support comes from a series of concrete footings called piers. Piers are positioned to distribute the weight of the deck and to provide intermittent support for the structural wood framework, which is perched above the ground to prevent decay. Because the

◀ The tool arsenal required for basic deck building is a modest one—a circular saw, a hand saw, a drill, a builder's level, a tape measure, and a hammer. Add a router, a jigsaw, and a power miter saw for greater accuracy, faster work, and more finishing details.

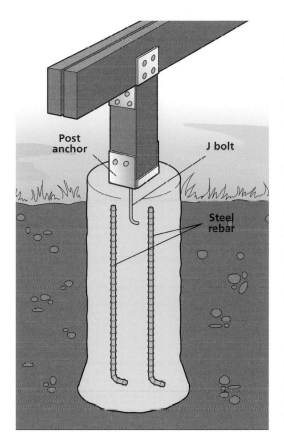

piers are set and poured independently, they provide design flexibility for unusual deck shapes or uneven terrain, something a flat concrete slab can't easily accommodate. The proper depth of the footings varies with climate and region; in general, the base of the concrete should always be below the frost line so the deck doesn't heave when the soil freezes. Most deck projects are governed by restrictions in the Uniform Building Code, so when you plan your project, check with your local building officials and ask about the construction requirements that apply. You can use the code guidelines to help plan the structural details of the deck, such as beam sizes and spans, to ensure safety and durability.

◄ The concrete pier footings for a deck carry all or most of the weight of the structure. Flaring the bottom to a larger diameter helps prevent settling; adding steel rebar helps prevent cracking and shifting due to lateral loads. A post anchor bolt is embedded in the top.

FREESTANDING DECK

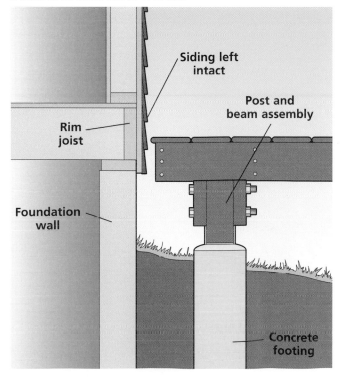

ATTACHED DECK

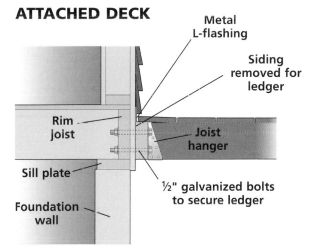

■ A concrete pier near the foundation supports the end of the freestanding deck (left), leaving a gap for water to drain. An attached ledger (above) needs flashing to shed water away from the home.

MATERIALS AND TECHNIQUES

If you want to include a deck as part of your outdoor kitchen project, but deck building is new to you, consult a more comprehensive guide such as *Better Homes & Gardens® Step-By-Step Deck Projects* or *Better Homes & Gardens® Complete Decks.* They provide a greater level of detail for all of the elements of deck construction, from piers to railings, but the following points will acquaint you with the fundamentals:

■ Use techniques similar to those shown for concrete slabs (see page 118) to lay out the size and shape of the deck. Consult a decking spans chart to ensure adequate strength. Mark pier locations that correspond to the post layout.

■ Use site-built wood forms or purchased cardboard tube forms to contain the concrete in each footing. Secure each form with stakes, wood braces, and screws.

■ Avoid burying the posts directly in the concrete footings; they are more likely to rot and the inevitable repairs will be more difficult. Instead insert a metal post base or an anchor bolt in the wet concrete so you can fasten a post on top of the footing.

■ Use only pressure-treated lumber for the structural framework of the deck—posts, beams, and joists. This is usually southern yellow pine

▶ Hex-head and carriage bolts, lag screws, and expansion anchors are used to fasten a deck frame together.

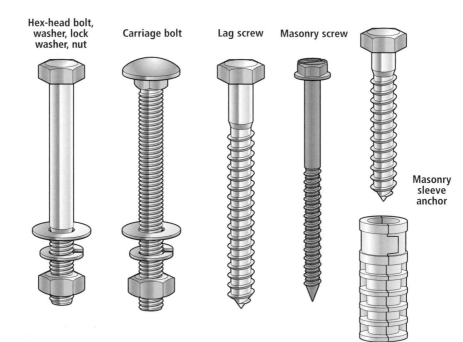

Hex-head bolt, washer, lock washer, nut

Carriage bolt

Lag screw

Masonry screw

Masonry sleeve anchor

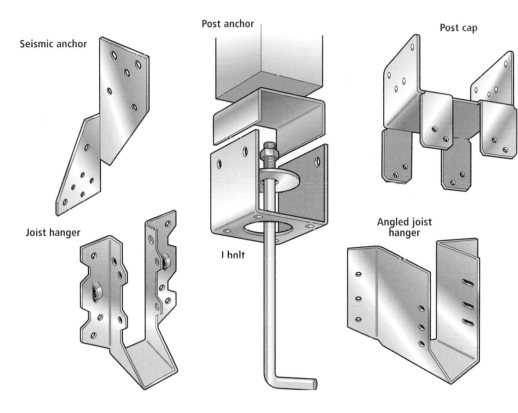

Seismic anchor

Post anchor

Post cap

Joist hanger

J bolt

Angled joist hanger

◄ Specialized metal framing brackets secure posts, beams, joists, and other structural deck parts. They provide faster, easier, and more secure joints than nailing or screwing framing members directly to each other.

that's been treated with a chemical preservative to ward off insect and moisture damage.

■ If you're building an attached deck, secure the ledger board directly to the house frame, not to the siding or sheathing. Use metal flashing to divert water away from the house-ledger connection.

■ Use steel framing connectors, such as joist hangers, and galvanized fasteners, such as nails, bolts, and lag screws, to connect the frame members. Hot-dipped galvanized hardware, with a thick, rough coating of zinc, provides better protection than electro-galvanized parts, which have a smoother finish. In oceanfront settings, use stainless-steel fasteners.

■ Decking planks can be made of solid lumber, engineered wood composites, vinyl, or even fiberglass. Wood species include pressure-treated pine, western redcedar, redwood, or exotic tropical species, such as teak or ipe. Engineered composites combine shredded wood fiber with plastic resins to create a uniform, rot-resistant material that needs little or no maintenance.

■ Local code requirements vary, but most require a 36-inch or higher railing on any deck platform more than 30 inches above the ground. Codes also specify the allowable gaps (almost always less than 4 inches) between the railing components. Building codes are put in place to ensure safe structures; be sure to follow them.

HIDDEN HARDWARE

To avoid the appearance of nailheads or screwheads in decking, use hidden fasteners, such as deck clips or a continuous rail. There is a price to pay for their cleaner appearance; these methods are more expensive and take longer to install. (See page 98 for another method.)

FINISHING TOUCHES

▶ This parquet decking pattern adds visual character to a simple design, and it is easy to build. The framing is not complicated and all the boards are the same length. Other more complicated patterns require additional framing for support; be sure to plan ahead.

COMMON DECKING PATTERNS

Single diagonal

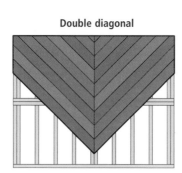

Double diagonal

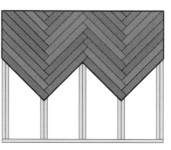

Herringbone

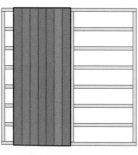

Perpendicular

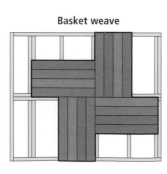

Basket weave

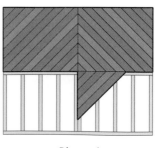

Diamond

▲ Introduce subtle design elements to a deck by changing the decking layout. Plan ahead for this by setting up the post locations and joist spacing you need for the decking pattern you want to use.

SAMPLE RAILING DESIGNS

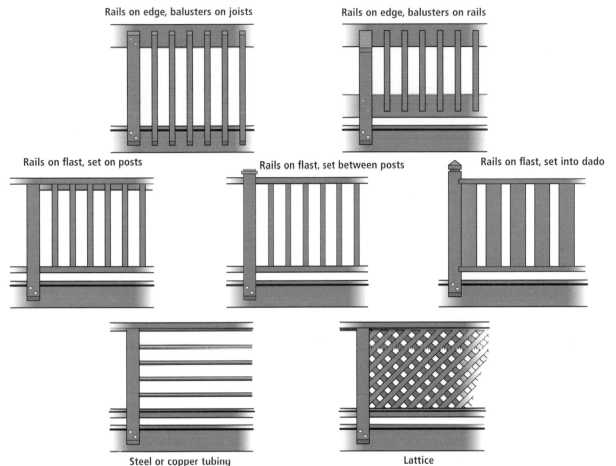

Rails on edge, balusters on joists

Rails on edge, balusters on rails

Rails on flast, set on posts

Rails on flast, set between posts

Rails on flast, set into dado

Steel or copper tubing

Lattice

▶ Deck railing construction can make use of wood, metal tubing, cable, engineered composite materials, or even tempered glass. Be sure to follow code guidelines for the size and spacing of parts.

FRAMING WITH WOOD

There's no arguing that masonry construction offers many advantages for building exterior structures, such as grilling stations or outdoor kitchens. It's fireproof, rot-proof, relatively affordable, and impervious to most kinds of water damage. Still, a wood or metal structural frame for your outdoor kitchen presents a viable option as well and opens up design possibilities you don't have with masonry.

Aside from the scale of the finished structure, basic framing techniques for a kitchen enclosure or workstation don't differ much from those used to build a house. You'll work mostly with nominal 2× dimensioned lumber to form lower and upper horizontal members called sills and plates, vertical members (studs), and a variety of other components (headers, trim studs, and blocking) used to frame openings for windows and doors. (See the illustration on the opposite page.) For more information, see *Better Homes & Gardens® Step-by-Step Basic Carpentry.*

Basic guidelines to follow:

■ For most outdoor projects, purchase pressure-treated lumber rather than standard framing lumber. Even though the frame won't likely be exposed to the elements, the rot- and insect-resistance of pressure-treated stock will add years of life to your project. (Earlier varieties of this lumber included arsenic in its chemical mix, but safer preservatives are now standard.)

■ For cabinets, build a separate base (also of pressure-treated lumber) for the structure to rest upon so the main sections don't sit directly on the ground where water and other hazards might degrade the materials.

■ Use hot-dipped galvanized nails to fasten the frame. The thick coating of zinc resists ordinary rust and the corrosive effects of preservatives in the lumber.

■ Place studs closer together, if necessary, to accommodate heavy loads, such as thick stone or concrete countertops. (Standard layout is studs at 16 inches center-to-center; 12 inches

▶ The materials, techniques, and skills needed to frame walls and cabinets for an outdoor kitchen are similar to those used in most remodeling projects.

BASIC WALL FRAME CONSTRUCTION

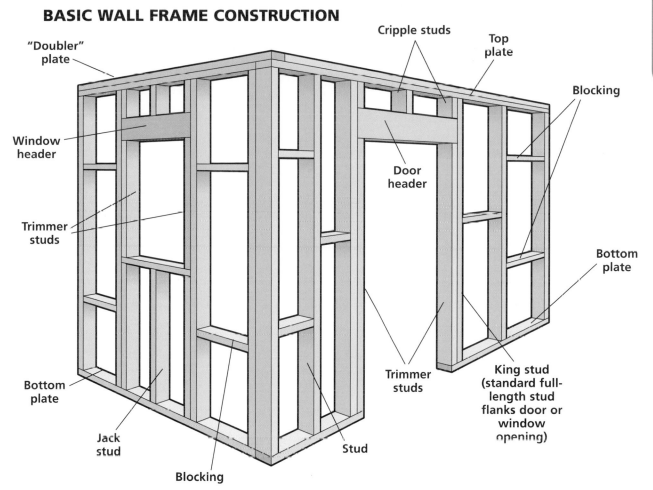

"Doubler" plate

Window header

Trimmer studs

Bottom plate

Jack stud

Blocking

Stud

Cripple studs

Top plate

Blocking

Door header

Bottom plate

Trimmer studs

King stud (standard full-length stud flanks door or window opening)

▲ Most outdoor kitchens won't require full-height walls, but the basic components shown here apply to smaller structures as well. Stud spacing is typically 16 inches on-center.

on-center will help support heavier weights.)

■ Use exterior plywood sheathing to add strength to the wall assemblies and prevent them from racking. If cement backerboard is necessary as a substrate for ceramic tile or stucco, fasten it over the plywood.

■ If you are installing a built-in grill, check the manufacturer's instructions on clearances required between the grill and combustible materials. Some grills are insulated and designed for zero-clearance installations; others may require a noncombustible barrier such as cement backerboard. If that's the case, you'll need to allow room for that material.

▼ A convenient substitute for large beam stock is a site-built header, which features a sandwich construction of 2× stock nailed together with ½-inch plywood in the center. The thickness is 3½ inches, the standard width of a 2×4 wall.

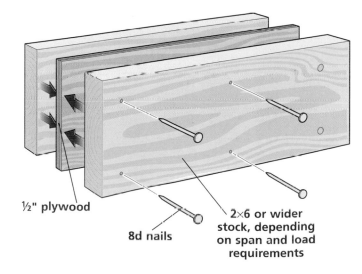

½" plywood

8d nails

2×6 or wider stock, depending on span and load requirements

LUMBER–NOMINAL VERSUS ACTUAL SIZES

In most cases lumber doesn't actually measure what the labeling indicates. That's because lumber sizes are stated in rough measurements, the way it used to be sold directly from the mill. Nowadays most lumber is dimensioned or milled to a smooth surface and a more consistent size, but the numeric designation is still that of a roughsawn board. For example, a 1×4 would actually measure ¾ inch thick by 3½ inches wide, and a 2×8 would typically measure 1½ inches thick by 7¼ inches wide. The sizes are fairly consistent to the industry standard, especially with boards from the same wholesale bundle or unit, but you need to calculate the actual and not the nominal dimensions when you are building with dimensioned lumber. Here are some common sizes:

NOMINAL SIZE	ACTUAL SIZE
1 x 4	¾" x 3½"
1 x 6	¾" x 5½"
1 x 8	¾" x 7¼"
2 x 4	1½" x 3½"
2 x 6	1½" x 5½"
2 x 8	1½" x 7¼"
2 x 10	1½" x 9¼"
2 x 12	1½" x 11¼"
4 x 4	3½" x 3½"
4 x 6	3½" x 5½"

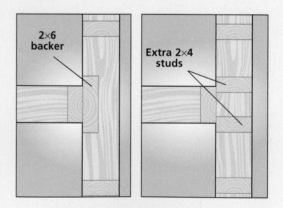

▶ Mid-wall intersections have to provide a strong wood-to-wood structural connection, plus a bearing surface for interior sheathing or drywall. Here are two common methods.

2×6 backer

Extra 2×4 studs

▼ Corner framing requires extra lumber if sheathing or drywall will be fastened to the inside faces of the wall. These examples represent three common variations.

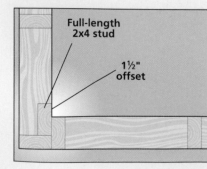
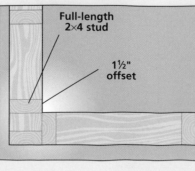
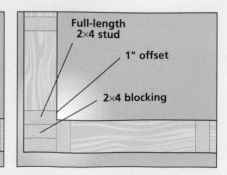

Full-length 2x4 stud

1½" offset

Full-length 2x4 stud

1½" offset

Full-length 2x4 stud

1" offset

2×4 blocking

FRAMING WITH METAL

Metal framing is increasingly common in both residential and commercial construction. For an outdoor kitchen it offers obvious advantages in resistance to insect and moisture damage. Though the tools and fastening techniques differ from those used with wood framing, the structural design principles are similar.

■ Consider the weight-bearing requirements before you build. Common metal framing components for residential use are fairly thin, typically about 25 gauge. Heavier gauge material (18 or 20 gauge) designed for commercial applications might be a better choice.

■ Rent a chop saw with an abrasive blade designed for cutting metal framing components. It's faster, safer, and more accurate than a portable circular saw fitted with a metal-cutting blade.

■ Oceanfront sites are not good candidates for metal framing, because the salt air is corrosive to steel. Use pressure-treated lumber in these areas.

■ Studs, box headers, and plate channels can be fastened together using sheet metal screws or rivets. As with wood framing, an entire wall section can be assembled and then installed as a single unit, using masonry anchors when securing to a concrete slab.

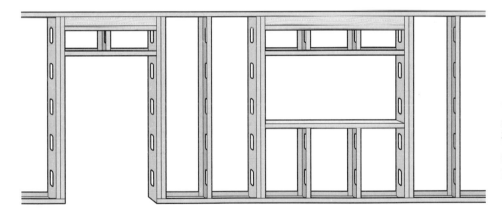

◀ Though header design is sometimes different, steel framing involves much the same layout as wood. The holes are for wire and pipe.

▼ Once the sill track is fastened in place, fit the studs one at a time. Set the stud in place at a slight angle and rotate it into position.

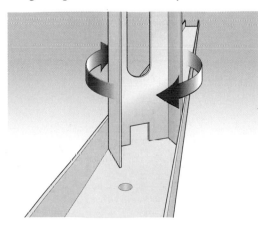

▼ Secure the metal framing connections with self-tapping sheet metal screws. Fasten wallboard with razor-point drywall screws.

UTILITY CONNECTIONS

Getting the most convenience and function from an outdoor kitchen typically means bringing water, gas, and electricity from the house. The decision to go this route can add significantly to the project cost, and in many cases it requires roughing in the utilities during the initial grading or site-prep work.

Living in a region where the ground freezes complicates the plan for a water-supply system. If the outdoor kitchen is detached from the house, the pipes need to run underground, buried in a trench 12 inches below the frost line. For areas where freezing isn't a concern, water pipes are buried 12 inches below grade. This may vary with local codes. Normally you cannot embed any horizontal run of pipe in concrete, and any vertical stems that come up through the concrete slab have to be wrapped with tape so they won't bind if the slab heaves.

Some installations involve specific material requirements as well. Plastic or galvanized-steel pipe can be used under certain cirumstances,

but lines that run under slabs typically have to be Type-L or -K copper, with soldered joints. (Type-M copper is a thin-walled pipe used in interior walls; don't use it for outdoor kitchens.)

Make sure you get approval for your plans from your local building department before this work is done. The same goes for the drain and vent lines; they are subject to numerous regulations. If your kitchen will feature a full supply and drain system for water, this part of the project should probably be hired out to a professional plumber. For more information on residential plumbing, see *Better Homes and Gardens® Step-By-Step Plumbing.*

For a low-tech approach that still provides convenience, install a prep sink in your outdoor kitchen and supply it with water from a garden hose. This requires a few standard pipe fittings, including a hose connection on the cooking center. You'll need a portable reservoir for grey water (a specialized 5-gallon container) placed inside the cooking-center base. This setup allows you to clean produce, wash your hands, or rinse

▶ Plumbing tools vary with the materials used. For plastic pipe, it's just a pipe wrench, a cutter, and glue. Copper requires a tubing cutter and a torch for soldering joints.

plates, and as long as you keep harsh cleansers or chemicals out of the sink, you can empty the waste water onto plants in your yard.

Making all these connections will be much simpler if you are attaching an outdoor kitchen directly to the house. In that case tying into existing water-supply and drain lines might still require a plumber's help, but it should be much easier—and less expensive—than roughing in new underground lines.

Gas connections

If you're going underground with water lines or electrical conduit, running a gas pipe for the grill and side burner won't complicate the project. Metal gas pipe must be buried a minimum of 12 inches; wrapped pipe and protected fittings or joints are often mandatory. If a gas line is to be buried under a concrete slab, a special-purpose gas conduit is usually required. Again, check with your local building official before you proceed.

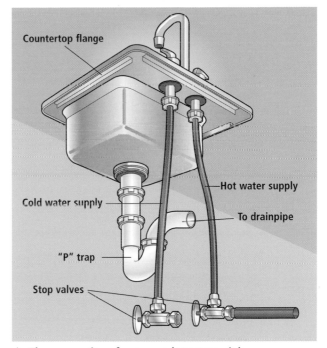

▲ The connections for an outdoor prep sink are the same those used indoors, but insulating wraps may be needed to protect pipes from freezing. In cold climates you'll need to drain the supply lines during the winter.

▲ Common materials for residential plumbing include copper pipe that requires soldered connections, brass supply lines, threaded steel pipe, PVC or ABS plastics, and cast iron.

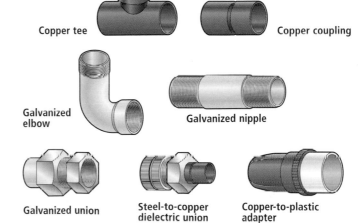

▲ Fittings connect lengths of pipe or let you switch from one kind of pipe to another. Some are slip fittings secured with glue or solder; others are threaded or have compression seals.

ELECTRICAL SERVICE

Electrical service for an outdoor kitchen not only adds the convenience and safety of adequate lighting, it also opens up options for having a refrigerator, an icemaker, a microwave oven, countertop appliances such as a blender, or a vent hood with a motorized fan. Unless you already have experience with residential electrical wiring, hire a licensed electrician for this work. This section will simply acquaint you with some of the common requirements and fittings for outdoor installations. For more detailed information on residential wiring, see *Better Homes and Gardens® Step-By-Step Wiring.*

An outdoor kitchen typically requires only one or two dedicated 20-amp, 120-volt circuits (an electric oven or cooktop burner may need a 240-volt circuit). If the service panel in your home doesn't have room for any more circuits, have a new subpanel added.

Like water and gas lines, electrical wiring for a detached kitchen must be buried underground and protected from damage. Minimum cover requirements (trench depth) range from as little as 6 inches for wires in rigid metal conduit to 24 inches for UF cable without conduit. Lines in plastic (PVC) conduit go 18 inches below grade. If there's a 4-inch or thicker patio slab above, most of these depth requirements are reduced. These codes are written as national standards and guidelines, and they may not be valid locally. Your local building officials can tell you what's required in your area.

Water and weather

The single biggest factor in outdoor installations is the safety concern of keeping the electrical ground path intact and preventing the flow of current into unintended conductors, such as metal appliances. Grounded electrical circuits

▶ The tools needed for basic electrical work are relatively few and simple. First is a wire stripping and cutting tool, but you'll also need assorted testers to check current, screwdrivers (a flat and a #2 Phillips), and a fish tape (not shown) if you're using conduit.

provide an escape path for runaway current. A ground connection diverts the current into the earth, tripping a circuit breaker back at the service panel. Without the ground, the current would travel through any conductor it could find, including you.

Unfortunately it's not always apparent if the ground path is intact, so special breakers or receptacles called ground fault circuit interruptors (GFCIs) must be used outdoors as a safeguard. They shut the circuit off immediately if the path to ground is interrupted. Outdoor switches, fixtures, and receptacles, as well as indoor fittings near water sources (in bathrooms and kitchens, for example), are required by law to have GFCI protection.

Water is an effective conductor of electricity, so outdoor fittings and fixtures sport gaskets, special covers, and other features to keep them dry. Some of the most common types are shown in the illustrations on this page. If you are not confident in your ability to handle the wiring required for your outdoor kitchen, hire a professional electrician.

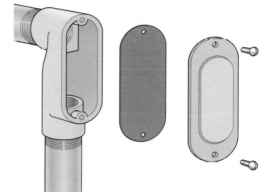

▲ Getting electricity to your outdoor kitchen will likely involve the use of underground conduit for the cable. Where the conduit goes underground and where it surfaces, fit access elbows to make running the wiring easier.

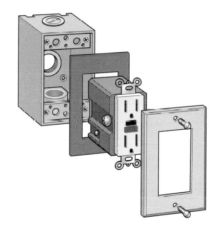

▲ Any outdoor electrical circuit must be protected with a ground fault circuit interruptor (GFCI). You can use a GFCI receptacle like the one shown here or add a GFCI circuit breaker at the panel.

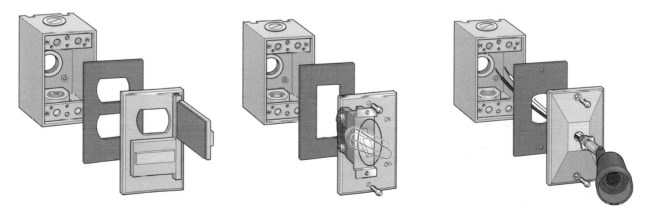

▲ Outdoor electrical fixtures and fittings typically feature special enclosures and gaskets to keep water away from the wiring. Shown here, from left to right, are a duplex receptacle box and cover, a switch box and cover, and a floodlamp socket with cover. Threaded ports in the boxes accept weathertight conduit fittings; unused holes are fitted with plugs.

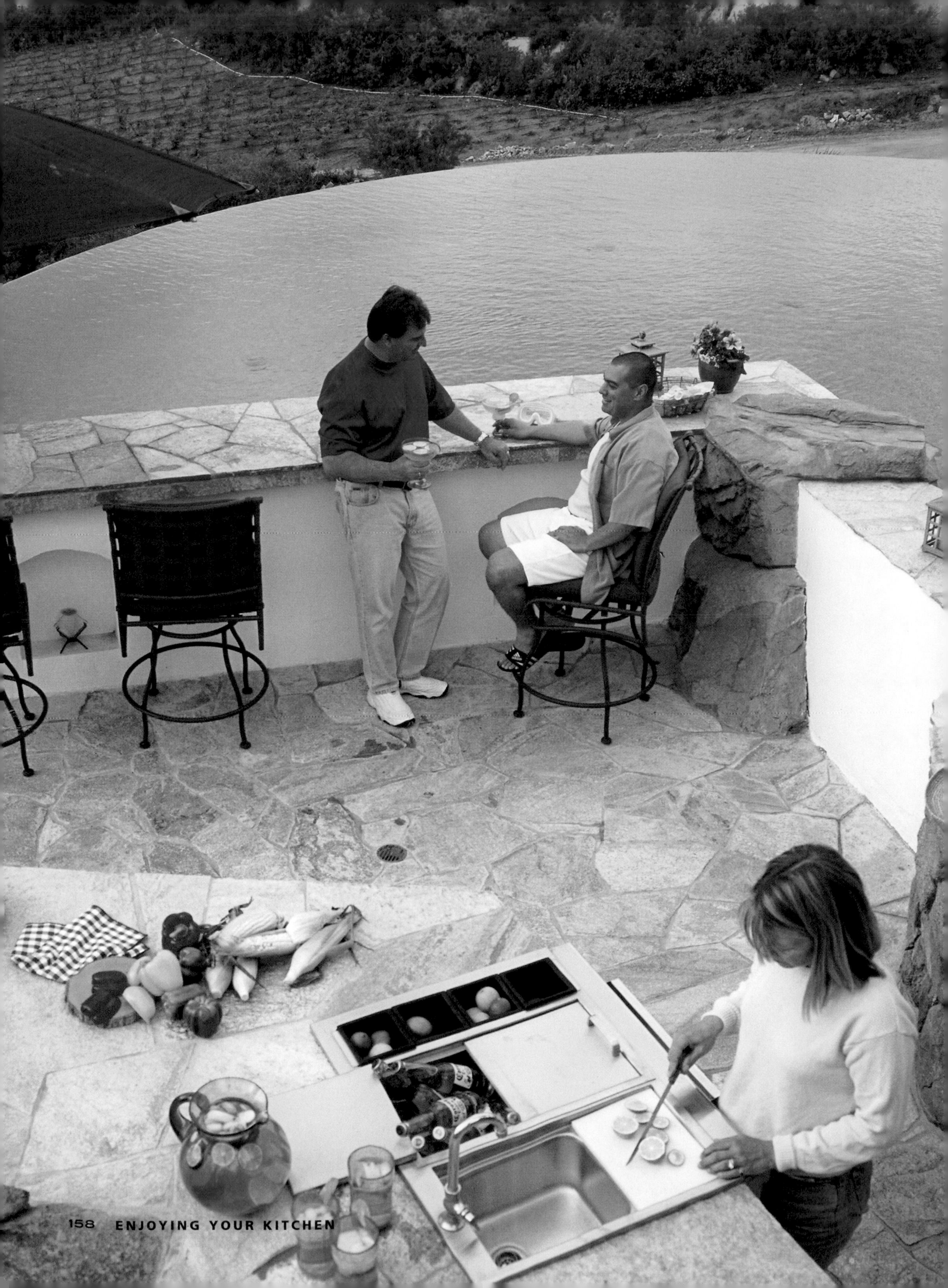

ENJOYING YOUR KITCHEN

Here's some refreshing news. After adhering to building code requirements and budget realities and the properties of the materials chosen for your outdoor kitchen, you have a lot more freedom in how you can actually use it. You can grill hot dogs, a prime cut of steak, or vegetables on skewers. Invite a hundred of your closest friends or indulge in a night of solitary dining. For dessert, savor a rich, smooth crème brûlée or just dunk cookies in cognac. But before all that freedom makes you giddy, keep in mind that ensuring years of great performance from your outdoor kitchen will require periodic care and maintenance. This applies to the grill first and foremost, but any outdoor appliance will need occasional inspection and cleaning, and the same goes for just about any exposed surface materials. That said, when the kitchen is finished it will be time for a well-deserved celebration—and as many dinners and get-togethers as you can fit in a season. This chapter provides an outline of the everyday care requirements of your kitchen, plus a section of proven recipes for simple but great-tasting foods perfect for outdoor cooking and dining.

CARE AND MAINTENANCE

Grill maintenance

Outdoor grilling introduces a few maintenance issues you won't encounter with most indoor cooking. Grills are relatively simple appliances, but without regular cleaning they can suffer from poor performance or dangerous flare-ups. The maintenance schedule can vary from two-month intervals for heavy use to as much as a year for a grill used only occasionally. Here are the basic elements to check:

■ **Cooking grates** – Care of the cooking grates depends on the type. Porcelain-coated steel should never be immersed in water, which creates cracking and scaling. A wet brass wire brush will remove the worst residue, but should be used only when the grates are cold. Cast-iron grates should be cleaned the same way; immersing them in hot soapy water does no harm, but you'll strip the "seasoning" (residue from cooking oils) off the grates. Stainless-steel grates should be cleaned with a fine steel-wool pad or a Scotch-Brite-type pad, with soapy water. Don't clean any grate when it's hot.

■ **Burner elements** – This is where the unseen problems tend to happen. Drippings and residue can clog burner holes, and spiders often clog the burner or valve by nesting inside or by leaving web residue behind. Spiders like the dark recesses of the burner and may be attracted by the smell of the unburned gas.

Whatever the reason, these creatures can wreak havoc by clogging the burner holes or valve. If the burner holes get clogged, for any reason, the likelihood of a dangerous flare-up increases, which can damage the grill and/or inflict burns on the user. To prevent problems, remove the burner and use a brush to clean out all the holes and the intake tube. This tube is a venturi valve with ports on the side where air enters to mix with the fuel. Flush the burner element with a garden hose after cleaning; this will reveal any plugged holes that need to be cleared. Infrared burners don't experience the same buildup of cooking grease, which is vaporized by heat. Ceramic briquettes–Simply turn them over to let the flame burn off the carbon buildup.

■ **Grill housing** – Painted housings should be cleaned only with dishwashing detergent or a household cleaner such as Formula 409, and a non-abrasive sponge or scrubbing pad. Stainless-steel housings can be cleaned with a solution of baby oil, dishwashing detergent, and water. If grease or carbon buildup is a problem, they can be scrubbed a little more vigorously and cleaned with degreasers (such as Simple Green) or sodium hydroxide cleaners (such as Speedy White), which dissolve crystallized carbon. Similar methods can be used on both inside and outside surfaces. Don't use caustic chemicals or oven cleaners.

Caring for outdoor surfaces

Materials used for outdoor projects are often chosen for their durability, but most need some routine maintenance to look their best and to hold up against the elements. As a general rule, if the material was placed in a liquid or semisolid form, it will require more care; grout, mortar, and concrete are good examples. These materials benefit from periodic applications of sealer to reduce moisture absorption. Unglazed tiles, brick, and porous natural stones such as slate require similar care. On countertops, denser stones such as granite or marble can get by with occasional applications of mineral oil.

▲ Sealers protect unglazed tile or porous stone as well as the grout joints. Water will stand on floors, however, so choose textured surfaces.

WHAT TO DO WITH WOOD

Though their use in outdoor kitchens is limited, wood surfaces tend to require more attention than the stone, masonry, and tile that comprise the bulk of outdoor building materials. Both sunlight and water are wood's natural enemies, so sealers make a huge difference. Clear penetrating finishes are easy to renew and can provide good protection against standing water and ultraviolet sunlight. Topcoats such as spar varnish or enamel paint offer the most protection but require more surface preparation and care in applying, especially for subsequent coats. To test the wood's condition, apply water. Beaded droplets indicate a properly sealed surface; if it soaks in, it's time to reseal.

Cooking in Your Outdoor Kitchen

Take the guesswork out of grilling by following these guidelines for lighting the fire and cooking in your new outdoor kitchen. Then turn to the collection of recipes for classic barbecue dishes plus a few innovations.

If you have a gas or electric grill, follow the directions in your owner's manual for lighting and preheating it. For gas grills, check to make sure you have enough fuel in the tank. The standard 20-pound propane tank gives 12 to 18 hours of nonstop grilling. Let a gas grill preheat for 10 to 15 minutes before you put the food on it. If the burners don't ignite on the first try, leave the grill open and turn off the gas. Wait about 5 minutes before trying again.

You have two basic choices for grilling: the direct method, which places foods directly over the heat source, and the indirect method, in which the food is cooked by heat trapped under the grill cover.

Direct grilling is best suited to foods that are tender, small, or thin, and can be cooked in less than 20 minutes. This includes steaks, burgers, kabobs, hot dogs, boneless poultry, fish, and most vegetables. To set up a gas grill for direct grilling, preheat it, then adjust the gas flow settings to the desired level. After you add the food, cover the grill with its lid. For a charcoal grill, use long-handled tongs to spread the coals evenly in a single layer. Leave the food uncovered.

Indirect grilling works well for cooking whole birds, ribs, large roasts, whole fish, and vegetables, such as potatoes and corn on the cob. With either gas or charcoal, you will need a drip pan, which collects the fat drippings from the foods and minimizes flare-ups. Use a disposable foil roasting pan or make one out of heavy-duty foil.

For a gas grill, light it according to your owner's manual, turn the setting to high, and let it preheat for 10 to 15 minutes. Reduce the heat on one burner to medium or medium-high and turn the other burner off. Place the drip pan on the lava rocks, ceramic briquettes, or flavorizer bars of the burner that's turned off. Adjust the gas to the burner that's on to maintain the desired temperature. Place the food on the grill rack directly over the pan.

For indirect cooking with charcoal, use long-handled tongs to arrange the hot coals around the drip pan. Place the food over the pan.

COOKING WITH CHARCOAL

When building a charcoal fire, place the coals on the bottom grate. There should be enough to cover an area about 3 inches larger on all sides than the size of the food you plan to cook. Add a few more briquettes if the weather is humid or windy. (It's always better to err on the side of too many coals versus too few.) Mound the briquettes or put them in a chimney starter and ignite them, leaving the grill lid off.

Instant-lighting briquettes, which ash over in about 20 minutes, are saturated with a petroleum product that lights easily with a match. In addition to electric starters and liquid lighter fluids, gels and paraffin fire starters are environmentally safe ways to make the job of lighting a charcoal fire easier. Wait about 1 minute after adding the liquid, gel, or wax starter before igniting the briquettes. Never use gasoline or kerosene as a fire starter.

After lighting the coals, keep them in a pile or in the chimney until they're glowing red (about 20 minutes), then spread them over the grate in a single layer. Let the coals burn for 5 to 10 minutes more (they will look ash gray in daylight or glowing red at night) before putting the food on the grill.

Adjusting the heat

If the coals are too hot, raise the grill rack, spread the coals apart, close the air vents halfway, or remove some of the briquettes. For a gas or electric grill, adjust the burner to a lower setting.

If the coals are too cool, use long-handled tongs to tap ashes off the burning coals, move the coals together, add briquettes, lower the rack, or open the air vents.

Everyone judges the temperature of coals differently. Therefore, the temperatures in the recipes are recommendations. For perfectly done food use the timings as guides and watch all foods on the grill closely.

Chile Pork Ribs with Chipotle Barbecue Sauce

These ribs get a powerful flavor boost from a dry rub plus a spunky barbecue sauce.

Prep: 15 minutes **Grill:** 1¼ hours **Makes:** 4 servings

  1 tablespoon cumin seeds, slightly crushed
  2 tablespoons brown sugar
  1 tablespoon chili powder
  1 teaspoon paprika
  ½ teaspoon ground red pepper
  ¼ teaspoon cracked black pepper
  3 to 4 pounds pork loin back ribs or
    meaty spareribs
  1½ cups bottled barbecue sauce
  ¼ cup finely chopped onion
  3 cloves garlic, minced
  ½ to 1 teaspoon finely chopped, drained
    chipotle pepper in adobo sauce

1. In a small skillet heat cumin seeds over low heat about 3 minutes or until toasted and fragrant, shaking skillet occasionally. Remove from heat; transfer to a small bowl. Stir in brown sugar, chili powder, paprika, red pepper, and black pepper. Trim fat from ribs. Use your fingers to rub spice mixt onto both sides of ribs.
2. For a charcoal grill, arrange medium-hot coals around a drip pan. Test for medium heat above the pan. Place ribs, bone sides down, on grill rack over drip pan. Cover and grill for 1 hour, adding more coals as necessary. (For a gas grill, preheat. Reduce heat to medium. Adjust for indirect cooking. Place ribs in roasting pan, place on grill rack, and grill as above.)
3. Meanwhile, for sauce, in a medium saucepan combine barbecue sauce, onion, garlic, and drained chipotle pepper in adobo sauce. Bring to boiling; reduce heat. Simmer, covered, for 10 minutes.
4. Continue grilling ribs for 15 to 30 minutes more or until ribs are tender, brushing occasionally with sauce. To serve, heat and pass any remaining sauce.

Nutrition Facts per serving: 446 calories, 17 g total fat (5 g sat. fat), 99 mg cholesterol, 883 mg sodium, 23 g carbohydrates, 2 g fiber, 49 g protein

Cast-Iron Skillet Cowboy Beans

Whether you make this over an open fire or on the latest state of the art grill, the bubbling satisfaction of a skillet full of beans can't be beat.

Prep: 15 minutes **Grill:** 30 minutes
Makes: 6 side-dish servings

  2 15-once cans pinto beans, rinsed and drained
  ½ cup chopped onion
  ½ cup catsup
  ½ cup hot strong coffee
  6 slices bacon, crisp-cooked, drained,
    and crumbled
  2 tablespoons Worcestershire sauce
  1 tablespoon brown sugar

1. In a 9-inch cast-iron skillet combine pinto beans, onion, catsup, coffee, bacon, Worcestershire sauce, and brown sugar.
2. For a charcoal grill, Grill beans in skillet on the rack of an uncovered grill directly over medium coals about 15 minutes or until bubbly. Grill for 15 to 20 minutes more or until beans are desired consistency, stirring occassionally. (For a gas grill, preheat grill. Reduce heat to medium. Place beans in skillet on grill rack over heat. Cover and grill as above.)

Nutrition Facts per serving: 184 calories, 4 g total fat (1 g sat. fat), 5 mg cholesterol, 1,003 mg sodium, 30 g carbohydrates, 8 g fiber, 9 g protein

COLORFUL KABOBS

Make these tempting kabobs with beef, chicken, or some of each.

Prep: 25 minutes. **Marinate:** 6 to 24 hours
Grill: 12 minutes **Makes:** 4 to 5 servings

> 1½ pounds beef sirloin steak, cut into 1-inch-thick pieces, and/or skinless, boneless chicken breasts and/or thighs
> ½ cup barbecue sauce
> ¼ cup water
> 2 to 4 cloves garlic, minced
> 2 tablespoons dried minced onion
> 2 tablespoons sugar
> 2 tablespoons steak sauce
> 2 tablespoons vinegar
> 2 tablespoons Worcestershire sauce
> 2 tablespoons cooking oil
> ½ teaspoon salt
> 2 medium onions, each cut into 8 wedges
> 10 to 12 medium mushrooms, stems removed
> 1 medium zucchini, halved and sliced ½ inch thick
> 1 large red or green sweet pepper, cut into 1-inch pieces

1. If using steak, trim off fat. Cut steak and/or chicken into 1-inch pieces. Place in a plastic bag set in a shallow dish.

2. For marinade, in a saucepan mix the barbecue sauce, water, garlic, dried minced onion, sugar, steak sauce, vinegar, Worcestershire sauce, oil, and salt. Bring just to boiling. Cool. Pour over steak or chicken; seal bag. Marinate in refrigerator for 6 to 8 hours or overnight.

3. In a saucepan cook onions, covered, in small amount of boiling water for 3 minutes. Add mushrooms; cook 1 minute. Drain. Thread onions, mushrooms, zucchini, and sweet pepper onto skewers.

4. Drain meat, reserving marinade; thread meat onto skewers. For a charcoal grill, cook on the rack of uncovered grill directly over medium coals for 12 to 14 minutes or until steak is desired doneness and chicken is no longer pink. Turn once halfway through grilling. In a saucepan, heat marinade until bubbly.

5. Grill vegetables over medium heat for 5 to 10 minutes, turning occasionally; brush with heated marinade. (For a gas grill, preheat. Reduce heat to medium. Place meat skewers, then vegetable skewers on grill rack over heat. Cover and grill as above.)

6. Serve immediately with warm marinade.

Nutrition Facts per serving: 372 calories, 18 g total fat (3-g sat. fat), 91 mg cholesterol, 652 mg sodium, 19 g carbohydrates, 3 g fiber, 34 g protein

HERBED ROASTED GARLIC SPREAD

In addition to spreading the roasted garlic over bread, you can mash it with potatoes, add to a vinaigrette, or toss with hot cooked pasta.

Prep: 20 minutes **Grill:** 35 minutes
Makes: 4 appetizer servings

> 4 garlic bulbs
> ¼ cup olive oil
> 1 teaspoon salt
> 1 teaspoon dried basil, crushed
> 1 teaspoon dried oregano, crushed
> ½ teaspoon pepper
> 8 slices sourdough bread, toasted and halved

1. With a sharp knife, cut off the top ½ inch from each garlic bulb to expose the ends of individual cloves. Leave garlic bulbs whole; remove any loose, papery outer layers.

2. Fold four 18×9-inch pieces of heavy foil in half to make 9-inch squares. Place each garlic bulb, cut side up, in center of a foil square. Drizzle the bulbs with olive oil and sprinkle with salt, basil, oregano, and pepper. Bring up opposite edges of foil and seal with a double fold. Fold the remaining edges together to enclose garlic, leaving space for steam to build.

3. For a charcoal grill, arrange medium-hot coals around a drip pan. Test for medium heat above the pan. Place foil packets with garlic on grill rack over drip pan. Cover and grill for 35 to 40 minutes or until garlic bulbs feel soft when packets are squeezed. Turn packets occasionally. (For a gas grill, preheat. Reduce heat to medium. Adjust heat for indirect cooking.)

4. To serve, unwrap garlic and transfer to serving plates. Squeeze garlic pulp from each clove; spread onto toasted bread.

Nutrition Facts per serving: 151 calories, 8 g total fat (1 g sat. fat), 0 mg cholesterol, 421 mg sodium, 18 g carbohydrates, 0 g fiber, 3 g protein

SALMON WITH FRESH PINEAPPLE SALSA

Enjoy the sweet-hot fruit salsa, sprinkled like confetti over this grilled salmon fillet. Serve it with hot cooked rice.

Prep: 20 minutes **Grill:** 12 minutes **Makes:** 4 servings

- 2 cups coarsely chopped fresh pineapple
- ½ cup chopped red sweet pepper
- ¼ cup finely chopped red onion
- 3 tablespoons lime juice
- 1 small fresh jalapeño pepper, seeded and finely chopped
- 1 tablespoon snipped fresh cilantro or chives
- 1 tablespoon honey
- 1 1-pound fresh skinless salmon fillet, 1 inch thick
- ¼ teaspoon ground cumin

1. For salsa, in a medium bowl combine pineapple, sweet pepper, onion, 2 tablespoons of the lime juice, the jalapeño pepper, cilantro, and honey. Set aside.

2. Rinse fish; pat dry. Brush both sides of fish with the remaining lime juice and sprinkle with cumin. Place fish in a well-greased wire grill basket. For a charcoal grill, cook fish on the rack, uncovered, directly over medium coals for 8 to 12 minutes or until fish flakes easily when tested with a fork. Turn basket once. (For a gas grill, preheat. Reduce heat to medium. Place fish in grill basket over heat. Cover and grill as above.) Cut fish into 4 serving-size pieces. Serve with the salsa.

Nutrition Facts per serving: 170 calories, 4 g total fat (1 g sat. fat), 20 mg cholesterol, 70 mg sodium, 17 g carbohydrates, 1 g fiber, 17 g protein

GRILLED SICILIAN-STYLE PIZZA

Traditional Sicilian cooking means greens sautéed with olive oil and served with bread to sop up the juices. Here's a grilled adaptation of that idea.

Prep: 20 minutes **Grill:** 8 minutes **Makes:** 4 servings

- 1 16-ounce Italian bread shell (Boboli)
- 2 roma tomatoes, thinly sliced
- 1 large yellow or red tomato, thinly sliced
- 4 ounces mozzarella cheese, thinly sliced
- ⅓ cup halved, pitted kalamata olives
- 1 tablespoon olive oil
- 1 cup coarsely chopped escarole or curly endive
- ¼ cup shredded Pecorino Romano or Parmesan cheese (1 ounce)
- Black pepper

1. Top bread shell with tomatoes, mozzarella cheese, and olives. Drizzle oil over all. Fold a 24×18-inch piece of heavy foil in half lengthwise. Place pizza on foil, turning edges of foil up to edge of pizza.

2. For a charcoal grill, arrange medium-hot coals around a drip pan. Test for medium heat above pan. Place pizza on the grill rack over the drip pan. Cover and grill about 8 minutes or until pizza is heated through, topping with escarole the last 2 minutes of grilling. (For a gas grill, preheat. Reduce heat to medium. Adjust for indirect cooking. Grill as above.) To serve, sprinkle cheese and freshly ground black pepper over pizza.

Nutrition Facts per serving: 459 calories, 19 g total fat (4 g sat. fat), 26 mg cholesterol, 893 mg sodium, 54 g carbohydrates, 3 g fiber, 24 g protein

STICKY-SLOPPY BARBECUE CHICKEN

Sherry lends uptown flavor to a down-home sauce.

Prep: 45 minutes **Marinate:** 2 to 4 hours
Grill: 50 minutes **Makes:** 6 servings

  3 to 4 pounds meaty chicken pieces (breasts, thighs, and drumsticks)
1½ cups dry sherry
  1 cup finely chopped onion
¼ cup lemon juice
  6 cloves garlic, minced
  2 bay leaves
  1 15-ounce can tomato puree
¼ cup honey
  3 tablespoons molasses
  1 teaspoon salt
½ teaspoon dried thyme, crushed
¼ to ½ teaspoon ground red pepper
¼ teaspoon black pepper
  2 tablespoons white vinegar

1. Place chicken in a plastic bag set in a shallow dish. For marinade, in a medium bowl stir together sherry, onion, lemon juice, garlic, and bay leaves. Pour over chicken; seal bag. Marinate in the refrigerator for 2 to 4 hours, turning bag occasionally. Drain chicken, reserving marinade. Cover and chill chicken until ready to grill.

2. For sauce, in a large saucepan combine the reserved marinade, the tomato puree, honey, molasses, salt, thyme, red pepper, and black pepper. Bring to boiling; reduce heat. Simmer, uncovered, about 30 minutes or until reduced to 2 cups. Remove from heat; remove bay leaves. Stir in vinegar.

3. For a charcoal grill, arrange medium-hot coals around a drip pan. Test for medium heat above the pan. Place chicken pieces, bone sides down, on grill rack over drip pan. Cover and grill for 50 to 60 minutes or until tender and no longer pink (180°F). Brush with some of the sauce during the last 15 minutes of grilling. (For a gas grill, preheat. Reduce heat to medium. Adjust for indirect cooking. Grill as above.) To serve, reheat and pass the remaining sauce with chicken.

Nutrition Facts per serving: 446 calories, 13 g total fat (4 g sat. fat), 104 mg cholesterol, 735 mg sodium, 33 g carbohydrates, 2 g fiber, 35 g protein

*CHILE PEPPERS contain volatile oils that can burn skin and eyes. Avoid direct contact with chiles as much as possible. When working with chile peppers, wear plastic or rubber gloves. If your bare hands do touch chile peppers, wash well with soap and water.

CORN WITH ANCHO-AVOCADO BUTTER

The velvety avocado butter melts in your mouth—corn on the cob never had it so good.

Prep: 25 minutes **Cook:** 5 minutes **Grill:** 10 minutes
Makes: 6 servings

½ to 1 small ancho chile pepper*
  2 tablespoons lime juice
  2 tablespoons water
  3 tablespoons butter or margarine, softened
½ of a small avocado, seeded, peeled, and chopped
⅛ teaspoon salt
  6 ears of corn with husks

1. For ancho avocado butter, in a small saucepan combine ancho chile pepper, lime juice, and water. Bring to boiling; reduce heat. Simmer, covered, over low heat about 10 minutes or until pepper turns soft. Drain; cool. Remove stems and seeds of pepper; finely chop pepper. In a small bowl combine pepper and butter. In another bowl slightly mash avocado with salt; stir into butter. Spoon into small mold or cup lined with plastic wrap; cover and chill.

2. Peel back corn husks, but do not remove. Take off corn silks. Rinse corn; pat dry. Fold husks back around cobs. Tie husk tops with 100-percent-cotton kitchen string.

3. For a charcoal grill, cook corn on the rack, uncovered, directly over medium coals for 10 minutes, turning several times. (For a gas grill, preheat. Reduce heat to medium. Place corn on grill rack over heat. Cover and grill as above.) Remove butter from mold. Remove plastic wrap. Serve corn with ancho-avocado butter.

Nutrition Facts per ear of corn with 2 tablespoons ancho-avocado butter: 246 calories, 10 g total fat (2 g sat. fat), 8 mg cholesterol, 125 mg sodium, 40 g carbohydrates, 6 g fiber, 5 g protein

ITALIAN SAUSAGE WITH SWEET & SOUR PEPPERS

For more Italian goodness, grill purchased polenta alongside the sausages and vegetables.

Prep: 20 minutes **Grill:** 10 minutes **Makes:** 6 servings

- 3 tablespoons slivered almonds
- ¼ cup raisins
- 3 tablespoons red wine vinegar
- 2 tablespoons sugar
- ¼ teaspoon salt
- ⅛ teaspoon black pepper
- 1 tablespoon olive oil
- 2 green sweet peppers, cut into 1-inch-wide strips
- 2 red sweet peppers, cut into 1-inch-wide strips
- 1 medium red onion, thickly sliced
- 6 sweet Italian sausage links

1. In a small nonstick skillet cook and stir almonds for 1 to 2 minutes or until golden brown. Stir in raisins. Remove skillet from heat. Let stand for 1 minute. Carefully stir in vinegar, sugar, salt, and black pepper. Return to heat; cook and stir just until the sugar dissolves.

2. Drizzle oil over sweet pepper strips and onion slices. Prick sausages several times with a fork. For a charcoal grill, cook vegetables and sausages on an uncovered rack directly over medium coals for 10 to 15 minutes or until no pink remains in the sausages and vegetables are tender. Turn once. (For a gas grill, preheat. Reduce heat to medium. Place vegetables and sausages on rack over heat. Cover and grill.)

3. In a large bowl toss vegetables with almond mixture; spoon onto serving platter. Place sausages on top.

Nutrition Facts per serving: 276 calories, 19 g total fat (6 g sat. fat), 59 mg cholesterol, 604 mg sodium, 15 g carbohydrates, 1 g fiber, 13 g protein

SUN-DRIED TOMATO BURGERS

Slather these tomato-studded burgers with a basil-mayonnaise dressing zipped up by a jalapeño pepper.

Prep: 15 minutes **Grill:** 14 minutes **Makes:** 4 servings

- 1 pound lean ground beef
- 1 tablespoon finely chopped, drained, oil-packed sun-dried tomatoes
- 1 teaspoon finely shredded lemon or lime peel
- ½ teaspoon salt
- ¼ teaspoon black pepper
- ¼ cup light mayonnaise dressing or salad dressing
- 2 tablespoons snipped fresh basil
- 1 jalapeño pepper, seeded and finely chopped
- 4 onion hamburger buns
- 1 cup lightly packed arugula or spinach leaves

1. In a medium bowl combine beef, tomatoes, lemon peel, salt, and black pepper; mix lightly but thoroughly. Shape into four ½-inch-thick patties. For a charcoal grill, cook patties on uncovered rack directly over medium coals for 14 to 18 minutes or until meat is done (160°F). Turn once halfway through grilling. (For a gas grill, preheat. Reduce heat to medium. Place patties on grill rack over heat. Cover and grill as above.)

2. Meanwhile, in a small bowl combine mayonnaise dressing, basil, and jalapeño pepper; mix well. For the last 1 to 2 minutes of grilling, place buns, cut sides down, on grill rack to toast. Top bottom halves of buns with burgers. Top with mayonnaise dressing mixture and arugula. Add bun tops.

Nutrition Facts per serving: 450 calories, 20 g total fat (6 g sat. fat), 71 mg cholesterol, 784 mg sodium, 40 g carbohydrates, 2 g fiber, 26 g protein

THAI-SPICED SCALLOPS

These tantalizing kabobs let you sample the whole spectrum of Thai flavors—sweet, sour, and spicy.

Prep: 20 minutes **Grill:** 20 minutes **Makes:** 4 servings

   1 **pound fresh or frozen sea scallops**
   2 **medium yellow summer squash and/or zucchini, quartered lengthwise and sliced ½ inch thick**
1½ **cups packaged peeled baby carrots**
   ⅔ **cup bottled sweet and sour sauce**
   2 **tablespoons snipped fresh basil**
   1 **teaspoon Thai seasoning or five-spice powder**
   ½ **teaspoon bottled minced garlic**

1. Thaw scallops, if frozen. Fold a 36×18-inch piece of heavy foil in half to make an 18-inch square. Place squash and carrots in center of foil. Sprinkle lightly with salt and pepper. Bring up 2 opposite edges of foil; seal with a double fold. Fold remaining ends to completely enclose the vegetables, leaving space for steam to build. For a charcoal grill, cook vegetables on uncovered rack directly over medium coals for 15 to 20 minutes or until vegetables are crisp-tender. Turn vegetables occasionally.

2. Meanwhile, for the sauce, in a small bowl combine the sweet and sour sauce, basil, Thai seasoning, and garlic. Transfer ¼ cup of the sauce to another bowl for basting. Reserve remaining sauce until ready to serve.

3. Rinse scallops; pat dry. Halve any large scallops. On four 8- to 10-inch skewers thread scallops. Place kabobs on grill rack next to vegetables; grill for 5 to 8 minutes or until scallops are opaque. Turn and brush once with basting sauce. (For a gas grill, preheat. Reduce heat to medium. Place vegetables, then scallops on rack over heat. Cover and grill.) Serve scallops and vegetables with remaining sauce.

Nutrition Facts per serving: 168 calories, 1 g total fat (0 g sat. fat), 34 mg cholesterol, 370 mg sodium, 25 g carbohydrates, 3 g fiber, 16 g protein

WARM ASPARAGUS, FENNEL, AND SPINACH SALAD

The components of this green-on-green salad distinguish themselves by taste: mild licorice-like fennel; a variety of mixed greens; and tender, smoky-sweet asparagus.

Prep: 15 minutes **Grill:** 12 minutes **Makes:** 4 servings

   1 **medium fennel bulb (about 1 pound)**
   2 **tablespoons water**
   2 **tablespoons olive oil**
   ¼ **teaspoon finely shredded lemon peel**
   4 **teaspoons lemon juice**
   ¼ **teaspoon salt**
   ¼ **teaspoon pepper**
   8 **ounces asparagus spears, trimmed**
   4 **cups fresh spinach**
   ¼ **cup shredded Parmesan cheese (1 ounce)**
   1 **tablespoon thinly sliced fresh basil**

1. Trim off stem end of fennel; quarter fennel but do not remove core. Place fennel in a small microwave-safe dish or pie plate. Add the water. Cover with vented plastic wrap. Microwave on high power (100%) about 4 minutes or until nearly tender; drain.

2. Meanwhile, for dressing, in a small bowl combine oil, lemon peel, lemon juice, salt, and pepper; whisk until smooth. Brush fennel and asparagus with 1 tablespoon of the dressing; set remaining dressing aside.

3. For a charcoal grill, cook fennel on uncovered rack directly over medium coals for 5 minutes. Turn occasionally. Add asparagus to the grill; cook the vegetables for 7 to 8 minutes more or until vegetables are tender. Turn occasionally. (For a gas grill, preheat. Reduce heat to medium. Place fennel, then asparagus on grill rack over heat. Cover and grill.)

4. Transfer fennel to a cutting board; cool slightly and slice into ¼- to ½-inch-thick slices, discarding core. Divide fennel and asparagus among 4 dinner plates. Arrange spinach on top. Drizzle with remaining dressing. Top with Parmesan cheese and basil.

Nutrition Facts per serving: 111 calories, 9 g total fat (1 g sat. fat), 5 mg cholesterol, 231 mg sodium, 5 g carbohydrates, 7 g fiber, 4 g protein

GLOSSARY

A-B

Air-entrainment The use of admixtures in concrete to create microscopic oxygen bubbles: The voids help protect the cured concrete against damage from freezing water.

Aggregate The non-cement solids used to make concrete. Crushed rock is the coarse aggregate; sand is the fine aggregate.

Backerboard A ready-made panel made with nylon mesh and a cement or gypsum core; used as a substrate for ceramic tile installations.

Backsplash The area directly above and behind a countertop. A backsplash can be an integral part of the countertop or fastened to the wall surface.

Batterboard A slat fastened horizontally to stakes at a foundation corner: Strings are run between batterboards to mark the perimeter of slabs or foundations.

Beam A large horizontal support member, often made of doubled 2× or 4× stock and secured to posts.

Bull float A wide flat tool approximately 3 feet long, fixed to a pole and used to float concrete slabs before troweling.

C-F

Casing The wood trim or moldings that surround a door or window opening.

Conduit Rigid or flexible tubing, made of metal or plastic, through which wires and cables are run. Often buried underground when used to convey electrical wire to an outdoor fixture.

Control joint A narrow groove cut or tooled into a concrete slab to prevent random cracking from shrinkage or stress. Depth is usually about one-fourth of the slab thickness, and joints are usually cut to form square proportions in the slab sections.

Flashing Thin metal barriers or layers, often preformed into bent shapes, used to divert water away from window and door openings and other interruptions in an exterior wall.

Floating The first step in finishing a concrete surface: Done before the bleed water appears, it seats the large aggregate below the surface and removes minor irregularities in flatness.

Footing A thick concrete support for walls and other structures; buried below the frost line to prevent heaving when the soil freezes.

Frost heave The lifting of a concrete slab or other structure from soil expansion due to freezing.

Frost line The maximum depth frost penetrates the soil during winter. This varies by region and determines the necessary depth for deck piers, foundations, and post footings.

G-L

Ground fault circuit interrupter (GFCI) An electrical safety device that senses shock hazards and automatically shuts off an electrical circuit. A GFCI can be a circuit breaker in the main panel or a special receptacle used in a kitchen, bathroom, or exterior setting.

Grout A thin mortar used to fill the joints between ceramic tiles; often colored to match or complement the tile.

Header The beam that spans the top of a door opening or window opening; often made by sandwiching two or more boards over a plywood core.

Jamb The top or side faces of a window opening or door opening. The top face is called the head jamb; the right and left sides are called the side jambs.

Joist A horizontal framing member, set on its edge and spanning an open space below, that supports a floor or ceiling.

Ledger A horizontal framing member fastened to a wall in order to support a floor frame or the joists in a deck structure.

M-P

Mastic A thick-bodied adhesive sometimes used to set ceramic tiles or other surfacing products such as resilient sheet flooring

Nippers Specialized pliers with chisel-like jaws, used to cut "bites" from ceramic tile.

Nominal dimension The stated dimensions of lumber or masonry components. In lumber, the nominal size reflects a rough-sawn product, so the dimensioned piece is smaller. Likewise in masonry units, the nominal size includes the mortar joint, so the brick or block alone is slightly smaller than stated.

On-center The term used to designate the distance from the center of one regularly spaced framing member to another, often kept uniform to allow for sheathing joints. Typical spacing is 16 inches for wall studs, floor joists, and rafters.

Pier A concrete pedestal that supports deck posts and other structural components. Usually set atop or cast as an integral part of a poured concrete footing.

Pressure-treated wood Lumber (typically southern yellow pine) that has been saturated with preservative compounds that resist insects and fungal decay. It is used for deck structures, sill plates, and other outdoor applications.

S-Z

Setback The distance from the edge of a structure to an adjacent property line, usually stated as a minimum requirement.

Slump The measure of concrete's consistency and/or tendency to flow when released from a test cone. The amount of vertical settling is called slump and is typically 5 to 6 inches for standard residential concrete.

Stucco A surface finish, often hand-applied or sprayed and then hand-troweled, that consists of two layers of mortar. It can be troweled smooth or imprinted with texture.

Substrate A foundation layer of material upon which another material is installed or fastened.

Thinset mortar A common setting adhesive for ceramic tiles, it's used to create a bonding layer between the substrate and tile.

Toenail To drive a nail at an angle to hold together two pieces of material.

Tuckpointing The process of refilling old masonry joints with new mortar.

Veneer A thin layer of decorative material, such as brick or stone, attached to the surface of a base material to serve as a facing.

Vitreous tile. Ceramic tiles with a low porosity, used indoors or outdoors, especially in wet locations such as a bathroom or patio.

INDEX

A-C

Access issues, 11

Angle iron, 52, 56, 130

Attached outdoor kitchens, 76–81, 100–105

Awnings, 76, 81, 100

Backerboard, 139

Backsplash, 80, 86

Batterboards, 95, 118

Bench, deck, 98

Brick

  countertop, 106–109

  courtyard kitchen project, 52–57

  patterns, 125

  paver patio, 108, 123–125

  veneer, 52–53, 56, 133

  walls, 134–137

Budget, 37

Building codes, 36

Built-in grilling station, 106–109

Cabinets, 78–79, 84–85

Cement backerboard, 56, 59, 61, 80, 92, 104, 139

Ceramic tile, 138–143

  backsplash, 142

  countertop, 24, 56, 61–62, 80, 92–93

  cutting, 141

  durability of, 138

  glaze, 24, 142, 143

  grouting, 142

  setting, 140–142

  spacers, 140

  substrate for, 138–139

  wall, application to, 93

  water absorption, 143

Charcoal, cooking with, 163

Cleanup, designing for, 29

Climate issues, 10, 18–19

Codes, building, 36

Concrete

  admixtures, 115, 116

  air entrainment, 115

  base preparation, 114, 118, 119

  block wall, 52–57, 64–69, 71–73, 88–92, 107–109, 126–133

  control joints, 116, 120, 121

  curing, 116, 122

  edging, 120, 121

  finishing tools, 115

  floating, 120–121

  footings, 54, 66, 95–96, 144–146

  forms, 69, 114–115, 119, 121

  ingredients, 114

  pouring a slab, 118–122

  reinforcement, 90, 114, 117, 119

  screeding, 120

  seats, 69

  slab anatomy, 112

  slump test, 115

  texture, 122

  troweling, 114, 121, 122

  volume, calculating, 116

  working with, 112–122

Contractors, working with, 35–37

Corners, squaring, 129

Countertops

  brick, 106–109

  ceramic tile, 24, 56, 61–62, 80, 92–93

  concrete block base, 56

  laminate, 24

  stainless steel, 24

  stone, 23, 86

Courtyard kitchen project, 52–57

D-F

Decks

  anatomy, 144

  bench, 98

  building basics, 144–149

  decking patterns, 148

  fasteners, 98

  footings, 95, 144–146

  frame, 96–98

  hardware, 146–147

  louvered wall attachment to, 60

  project plan, 94–99

  railings, 98, 149

  for uneven terrain, 18

Design. *See also* Planning

  cleanup, 29

  cooking, 26–27

  dining, 28

  food preparation area, 23–25

  principles, 20–21

  process, 30–31

  professional help, 35

  storage, 22–23

  work triangle, 21

Design idea gallery, 38–49

  Classical Gas, 42

  Family Oasis, 41

  Fiesta Colors, 40

  Gimme Shelter, 46–47

  Heat Is On, 44

  Hideaway Haven, 43

  Island, 45

  Staying Connected, 48–49

Dining
  arrangements, 28
  poolside, 76–81
Drain lines, 90, 154–155
Dry well, 90
Efflorescence, 137
Electrical service, 156–157
Fire pit, 27, 70–71, 74–75
Fireplace, 64, 68
Fittings, 155
Flagstone, 71–73, 87
Flare-ups, controlling, 166
Food. See Recipes
Food preparation area, design of, 23–25
Footings
  deck, 95, 144–146
  wall, 54, 66
Framing, 63, 103–104, 150–153
Framing brackets, 147

G-O

Gas connections, 155
Gazebo, 82–85
Glulams, 62
Granite countertop, 23, 86
Grates, cooking, 33–34, 160
Grills, 32–34
  accessories, 34
  capacity, 34
  costs, 34
  direct vs. indirect grilling, 162–163
  fuel, 26, 32
  hardware, 32–33
  insulation, 59, 61, 104
  maintenance, 160
  ventilation, 26, 80

Grouting tile, 142
Hardware, deck, 146–147
Header, 151, 153
Insulation, grills, 59, 61, 104
Ipe (hardwood), 94–99
Knee boards, 122, 124
Laminate countertop, 24
Layout creation, 14–16
Location, 17
Loggia, 70–75
Louvered wall, 59
Lumber
  deck, 146–147
  framing, 150–152
  glulams, 62
  sizes, nominal versus actual, 152
Maintenance, grill, 160
Metal, framing with, 153
Mortar
  for backerboard joints, 139
  for brick wall, 134–137
  for ceramic tile, 139–141
  for concrete block walls, 91–92, 128–131
  curing, 137, 142
  for flagstone, 72–73, 87
  removing residue, 136, 137
  stucco, 132
  thinset, 80, 92–93, 139–141
  tooling joints, 131
  tuck pointing, 137
Muriatic acid, 137
Needs, assessment of, 7–11
Nippers, tile, 141
Oven, wood-burning, 27

P-S

Patio
  brick paver, 108, 123–125
  flagstone, 87
Pavers, 108, 123–125
Piers, 60, 95, 144–146
Pipe, 154–155
Planning, 7–37
  access, 11
  cleanup, 29
  climate, 18–19
  contractors, working with, 35–37
  cooking, 26–27
  design principles, 20–21
  design process, 30–31
  dining, 28
  food preparation area, 23–25
  layout creation, 14–15
  location, 17
  product guide, 32–34
  site checklist, 19
  site evaluation, 16
  size, 8
  storage, 22–23
  terrain, 18
  type of cooking, 9
  weather, 10
Planter wall, 64–69
Plumbing, 154–155
Poolside dining project, 76–81
Projects
  All the Angles, 88–93
  Basic Built-in, 106–109
  Under the Big Top, 58–63
  Classic Brick Courtyard, 52–57
  Dining Center Stage, 82–87
  Fire and Shelter, 70–75

Gimme Shelter, 100–105

Out in the Woods, 94–99

Poolside Dining, 76–81

Rock Solid, 64–69

Quartz countertop, 23

Railings, deck, 98, 149

Recipes

Chile Pork Ribs with Chipotle Barbecue Sauce, 164

Colorful Kabobs, 165

Corn with Ancho-Avocado Butter, 165

Grilled Sicilian-Style Pizza, 166

Herbed Roasted Garlic Spread, 167

Italian Sausage with Sweet & Sour Peppers, 168

Salmon with Fresh Pineapple Salsa, 166

Sticky-Sloppy Barbecue Chicken, 167

Sun-Dried Tomato Burgers, 168

Thai-Spiced Scallops, 169

Warm Asparagus, Fennel, and Spinach Salad, 169

Refrigerator, 22, 93

Reinforcement, steel

for concrete block walls, 52, 54–55, 66–67, 127, 130

for concrete slabs, 90, 117, 119

Roof, fabric, 58, 62–63

Saws, 141, 153

Screeding, 120, 123, 125

Sink, 20, 25, 29, 154–155

Site checklist, 19

Site evaluation, 16

Size, 8

Squaring corners, 129

Stone

countertop, 23–24, 86

veneer, 64–68, 83, 133

Storage, 22–23, 86–87

Story pole, 136, 137

Stucco, 71–74, 132

T-W

Taping backerboard joints, 139

Thermometer, food, 167

Tile. *See* Ceramic tile

Tuck pointing, 137

Universal design issues, 11

Utility connections, 154–157

building codes, 154

electrical, 156–157

gas, 155

water, 154–155

Veneer, 52–53, 56, 64–67, 83, 133

Vent hood, 26, 80

Walls

brick, 134–137

concrete block, 52–57, 64–69, 71–73, 88–92, 107–109, 126–133

for dining loggia, 70–73

foundation, 127

framing, 103–104, 151–153

louvered, 59

planter, 64–69

retaining, 54, 64, 66

stucco application to, 71–74, 132

veneer, 52–53, 56, 64–67, 133

Water supply, 25, 154–155

Weather issues, 10, 18–19

Work triangle, 21

RESOURCES

American-Made Awnings
P.O. Box 310
Dekalb TX 75559
800/789-1212
americanmadeawnings.com

Big Green Egg
3414 Clairmont Rd.
Atlanta GA 30319
404/321-4658
biggreenegg.com

Bull Outdoor Products, Inc.
541 E. Main St
Ontario CA 91761
800/521-2855
www.bullbbq.com

Cabana Kitchens
P.O. Box 510
1801 Pine Tree Drive
Buford GA 30515
678/482-9258
cabanakitchens.com
e-mail: info@cabanakitchens.com

Coleman
800/835-3278
coleman.com

Crown-Verity, Inc.
37 Adams Blvd.
Brantford, Ontario CANADA
519/751-1800
crownverity.com

DCS (Dynamic Cooking Systems)
5800 Skylab Rd.
Huntington Beach, CA 92647
800/433-8466
dcsappliances.com

Dacor
1440 Bridge Gate Drive
Diamond Bar, CA 91765
800/793-0093
www.dacor.com

Ducane Gas Grills
800 Dutch Square Blvd. Suite 200
Columbia SC 29210
800/DUCANES
www.ducane.com

Dynasty/Jade Products Co.
7355 E. Slauson Ave.
Commerce CA 90040
800/462-9824
dynastyrange.com

Electri-Chef
800/442-7207
electrichef.com

GE Answer Center®
800/626-2000
www.geappliances.com

Harbor Island Outdoor Living
1240 Eastwood Rd
Wilmington NC 28403
910/256-0459
harborislandoutdoorliving.com

HastyBake
7656 East 46th Street
Tulsa OK 74145
800/426-6836

Kitchenaid
800/422-1230
www.kitchenaid.com

Lynx Professional Grills
6023 East Bandini Blvd.
Commerce CA 90040
323/838-1770
www.lynxprofessionalgrills.com

Marvel Industries
P.O. Box 997
Richmond IN 47375-0997
800/962-2521
marvelindusries.com

MHP (Modern Home Products)
150 South Ram Rd.
Antioch IL 60002
888/647-4745
modernhomeproducts.com

P.E.S. Equipment
3768 S. 300 West
Salt Lake City UT 84115
800/841-6408
pcsequipment.com

PGS (Pacific Gas Specialties Corporation)
2641 DuBridge Ave., P.O. Box 16097
Irvine CA 92623-6097
949/757-7723
pgscorp.com

Sears, Roebuck & Co.
Sears.com

Solex Exterior Shadings
950 Quality Drive
Lancaster SC 29720
888/901-2522
solexshadings.com

Sunbeam Products, Inc.
800/200-2300
sunbeam.com

Sunesta Products
11320 Distribution Ave. East
Jacksonville FL 32256
904/268-8000
sunesta.com

Sunsetter Products
184 Charles Street
Malden MA 02148
800/876-2340
sunsetter.com

Texas Pit Master, Inc.
31903 State Hwy. 249
Tomball TX 77275
877/697-7487
e-mail: sales@texaspitmasters.com

The Grill Store & More
5715 Jones Creek Rd.
Baton Rouge LA 70817
877/743-2269
thegrillstoreandmore.com

Thermador
800/656-9226
www.thermador.com

Vermont Islands
279 River Road South
Putney VT 05346
866/345-4541
vermontislands.com

Viking Range Corporation
111 Front Street
Greenwood MS 38390
888/VIKING1
www.vikingrange.com

Weber-Stephens Products Co.
200 East Daniels Road
Palatine IL 60067-6266
800/446-1071
www.weber.com

Wolf Steel Ltd.
24 Napoleon Rd.
Ontario CANADA
705/721-1212
napoleongrills.com